"From the life of Jesus, the master teacher, Sr. Melannie has gleaned many lessons that any teacher can appreciate. Not only does her book offer background information for Mark's Gospel and insightful interpretations, but it is sprinkled with delightful comments. The prayers to Jesus in response to the Scripture passages are thought-provoking. Teachers today will find Sr. Melannie's book in tune with their mind and hearts."

Mary Kathleen Glavich, S.N.D.
Author, *Discipline Made Easy*

"When it comes to catechists, we often pay attention to their grasp of content and teaching skills. In *Jesus, I'm a Teacher, Too!*, Sr. Melannie pays attention to their spirituality! I especially like the fact that this book is so Jesus-centered! There's nothing more important to a catechist than to develop his or her relationship with the Lord. *Jesus, I'm a Teacher, Too!* encourages catechists to spend time talking with the Lord. I can think of no better formation than that!"

Joe Paprocki
Author, *Empowering the Catechist*

"In *Jesus, I'm a Teacher, Too!* Sr. Melannie Svoboda offers teachers and catechists an introduction to Jesus as he is seen in the gospel of Mark. Each reflection recalls that Jesus was a teacher who encountered some of the real day-to-day challenges of teaching, for example, lesson plans that go awry and students who don't respond."

Barbara Gargiulo
Teacher and Catechist

"Teachers, teacher aides, and volunteer catechists will all find this book inspiring, challenging, and comforting. We are reminded that Jesus, too, had his problem students, his bad days, his interrupted lessons, and his star pupils. Anyone who has ever stood in front of a roomful of students will delight in these meditations and conversations with Jesus."

Peg Bowman
Author, *At Home with the Sacraments*

"Sr. Melannie has a special talent for bridging the gap between the first century and today. An experienced teacher herself, she is also able to recognize and express clearly the implications of Jesus' message for contemporary teachers and students."

Demetrius Dumm, O.S.B.

"Sr. Melannie effectively prays the Gospel of Mark, from beginning to end, as a teacher. She reflects on these verses with the real feelings that teachers experience concerning the nitty-gritty of every-day teaching. I recommend that teachers and catechists use one reflection each week, creating a practical but personal theme that will hold each week together."

Dr. Greg Dues, DRE,
Pastoral Associate, Author

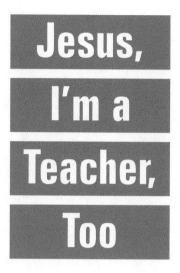

Jesus, I'm a Teacher, Too

*Guidance and Inspiration
from the Gospels*

Melannie Svoboda, S.N.D.

TWENTY-THIRD PUBLICATIONS
Mystic, CT 06355

Second printing 1997

Twenty-Third Publications
185 Willow Street
P.O. Box 180
Mystic, CT 06355
(860) 536-2611
800-321-0411

ISBN 0-89622-645-X
Library of Congress Catalog Card Number 94-62049
Printed in the U.S.A.

Dedication

To the Sisters of Notre Dame
of Chardon, Ohio
my teachers, my sisters,
my colleagues, my friends

Preface

Jesus was called many things in his lifetime: healer, prophet, savior, king, Messiah. But the title most frequently used for him was rabbi, that is, teacher. This book, based on readings from the Gospel of St. Mark, focuses on Jesus as teacher. Each chapter begins with a scripture reference and a significant line from that particular passage. I encourage catechists and teachers to read the gospel passage itself before reading the reflection. The reflection offers a few thoughts on the passage and relates it to the ministry of teaching. I conclude each chapter with a prayer to Jesus that flows directly from the gospel and the reflection.

This book can be used for personal prayer and reflection by an individual teacher or catechist. It can also be used for catechist or faculty prayer services, or for group sharing.

Now let us follow Mark's story of Jesus the teacher from the shores of the Jordan River to the door of that empty tomb.

Contents

Introduction

Jesus, I'm a Teacher, Too

Jesus, I'm a teacher, too. And although there are certainly differences in our teaching situations, there are some striking similarities.

There are differences. Your students were older than mine—your twelve apostles, the scribes and Pharisees who challenged you, the crowds that sat mesmerized at your feet—almost all of them were adults. My students are mostly kids. Just kids. Yet I believe that, despite the difference in their ages, our students share many things in common. And so you and I share many things in common.

For one thing, we've both experienced eager students—those who are genuinely happy to be in class, who get excited about learning, and who sometimes stay after class to help out or just to talk. You had your twelve apostles. You also had a Zacchaeus, who was so eager to have you as a teacher that he climbed up a sycamore tree just to get a glimpse of you. And you had a Nicodemus, who stayed after school well into the night to ask you more questions about the lesson you were teaching. I've had my share of eager students, too, Jesus. We both know that such students inspire us to teach well, to teach better, or to even teach at all. We thank "Abba" for them, don't we? We never take them for granted. Nor do we harbor unrealistic expectations that all our students should somehow be like them.

You and I have difficult students, too, Jesus. Students who are reluctant to learn or even downright antagonistic toward learning, and sometimes toward us. They come to class dragging their feet—or sometimes they don't come at all. They're bored with learning. After all, they know it all already—or they know as much as they've decided they want to know. They don't do their homework, they don't pay attention, and they constantly act up. I've had my difficult students, Jesus, as you've had yours. Take the Pharisees, those "religion-know-it-all's," whose initial curiosity with you eventually festered into a hatred so great that they had to kill you. Then there was Judas—one of your honor students. He sat in your class day after day, appearing to take all your lessons to heart, when in reality he was gathering enough evidence against you to justify betraying you.

Even your better students, your apostles, tried your patience and let you down at times by continuously missing the point of your stories and lessons. You taught forgiveness and they asked, "But there's a limit, isn't there?" You taught love of neighbor and they interjected, "Sure, but that means only my friend next door, right?" You told them that suffering and death lay ahead for you in Jerusalem and they responded, "Then let's not go there!" How frustrated you must have been at times, Jesus—like I am at times. Yet you didn't throw up your arms in disgust and walk away. You kept teaching, day after day. Sometimes the same lessons, over and over. Like I do.

Jesus, let me learn from you. Let me walk with you through the pages of the Gospel of St. Mark. Let me hear your words anew; let me see your deeds afresh. May they speak directly to me—to my heart. And may they inspire me to speak directly to you—from my heart.

Jesus, I want to learn from you, for I'm a teacher, too. Amen.

1. John the Baptist

John the Baptist appeared in the desert. . . .

Mark 1:4–8

Reflection

What a character John the Baptist was: dramatic, rough, strange, even a little weird. He was something of an extremist, that's for sure. Yet what a highly effective preacher he was. His teaching of repentance, not a particularly attractive topic in any age, was nonetheless popular with the people. Why? It definitely wasn't due to any suavity or slick salesmanship on his part—this guy had none of that. He lived in caves. He wore funny clothes. He ate bugs, for heaven's sake! He was anything but debonair.

Then what accounts for his extraordinary appeal? Maybe it was his sincerity—John definitely had that. His actions coincided with his words; his behavior and lifestyle were in perfect agreement with his teachings. That's sincerity. John believed: If you teach repentance, you yourself must repent; if you teach austerity, you must be austere. It was as simple (or as difficult) as that.

It's the same for us as teachers. Our students will look for sincerity in us. They will study us intently to see if we're actually living up to what we're teaching. And if we are, then they will be more apt to listen to us. For as Pope Paul VI wrote, "People listen more willingly to witnesses than to teachers."

Maybe John's success was also due to his humility. To the crowds that flocked to hear him, he unashamedly admitted, "One mightier than I is coming after me." Though popular himself, he directed the people's attention to someone other than himself. Years ago Frank Sheed told a group of teachers this: "Make up your mind whether you are preaching Christ or yourself. If it's yourself, heaven help you. For the better you do it, the worse it is."

John had good old-fashioned zeal, too. He boldly proclaimed the message God inspired him to speak. He went to where he felt God was calling him to go. He put in long hours. He poured himself out. In short, John channeled his time and energy into a cause he believed in. He gave it his all. And the people noticed. In fact, they began to believe in what he stood for.

John the Baptist: dramatic and strange, yes, but sincere, humble, and full of zeal, too. Little wonder he was such a good preacher.

Prayer

Jesus, your cousin John attracts and bothers me. He attracts me by his energy and his zeal. Would that I could be like that when I teach—so on fire, so certain, so free of all that encumbers.

But John bothers me, too. He unsettles me. He is a person who incarnates his convictions, who practices what he preaches. And that causes me to raise questions about my own way of living and teaching. Does my lifestyle reflect what I preach to my students? Do my daily choices mirror my daily lesson plans? Does my behavior incarnate my religious beliefs?

Jesus, help me to be more like John. Increase my sincerity, humility, and zeal. Help me to continue to channel my time and energy into a cause I truly believe in: educating the big and little people of God. Amen.

2. About Beginnings

It happened in those days that Jesus . . . was baptized in the Jordan.   Mark 1:9–11

Reflection

Beginnings can be hard. But they can also be exciting. There is a certain thrill in taking that first step, in embarking on a new venture, in laying the foundation.

The baptism of Jesus was a beginning. It was the beginning of Jesus' public ministry. For thirty-some years he had lived a rather unassuming and private life in Nazareth. Tradition tells us he was probably a simple carpenter. The baptism marked a dramatic change for him. It signified an end to a relatively tranquil life and the beginning of a decidedly hectic one.

We can only guess what Jesus was feeling at this moment. Maybe he was excited. Or perhaps he experienced a certain tinge of apprehension. Although Mark doesn't tell us what Jesus was experiencing inwardly at this moment, he does tell us what he was experiencing outwardly. The heavens were "torn open;" the Spirit descended upon him "like a dove," the voice of God "came from the heavens" and said to Jesus, "You are my beloved Son." Jesus was affirmed by God as he began his new mission in life. God called him "beloved." What better send-off could Jesus have gotten?

The dove that descended upon Jesus was a symbol of peace. It was a sign that Jesus' ministry would not be characterized by brute force or violence, but by peace and gentle love.

As teachers and catechists, our lives can be hectic at times. They can be too public for comfort. Our busyness and availability can cause fatigue or bring discouragement. But hopefully we have experienced in some way the same kind of affirmation by God that Jesus experienced at his baptism—the firm conviction that we are "beloved" by God. Such a conviction excites and energizes us. It also brings us deep peace.

Prayer

Jesus, about beginnings . . . Your baptism marked a beginning for you. I know something about beginnings. I know something about the excitement that often accompanies them—as well as the apprehension. I usually experience both at the start of something new—whether it be a new job, a new school year, a new unit, or just a new day.

But the words God spoke to you at your baptism are important for me to remember. For they gave you both a clarification of your identity and a dose of heavenly encouragement. (Sometimes I could use both!) The words told you who you were—God's son. More importantly, they told you that you were God's *beloved* son. They reminded you that you were not ministering alone.

Jesus, let me hear those same words being spoken now to me: "You, are my beloved child. In you I am well pleased." May my ministry of teaching, like yours, be characterized by peace and gentle love. For I know that you are with me in my teaching—the whole way—from beginning to end! Amen.

3. About Temptation

*The Spirit drove him out into the desert, and he re-
mained in the desert for forty days, tempted by Satan.*

Mark: 1:12–13

Reflection

There is a Hasidic saying that goes like this: "God is not
nice. God is not an uncle. God is an earthquake." These
words seem to apply to the above brief passage from Mark.
For no sooner had Jesus been affirmed by God at his baptism, than he was driven by the Spirit of God into the desert.
In other words, no sooner had he been commissioned by
God, than he was thrown into combat with the devil.

Something interesting was going on here. Oftentimes we
think of temptation as evil; however, this passage sheds a
different light on it. Temptation may be difficult, terribly
uncomfortable, and even downright embarrassing, but it is
not evil. Even Jesus had to face his share of temptations—
right from the beginning. Jesus' ministry was not going to
be a carefree stroll through a rose garden. No, Jesus' mission, not unlike our own, was going to involve serious
temptation and profound struggles with the forces of evil.

Mark says, "He was among wild beasts," and we might
be thinking, "That describes me in the classroom!" For we
all have days when our students seem uncontrollable and
truly on the "wild" side. But the phrase "wild beasts" could
also represent the temptations we meet regularly in our
teaching. Sometimes the temptations are small. Instead of
preparing well for a class, we decide to "wing it." Instead
of really listening to our students, we cut them off with a

quick "Yes, but. . . !" At other times the temptations will be bigger ones. We'll be tempted to treat a student unfairly, to pass on hurtful gossip about another, or to quit teaching altogether.

In this temptation narrative, Jesus was the victor, but we know his struggles with Satan were far from over. Throughout his ministry he would wage war with evil forces again and again. Mark added an interesting detail at the end: "The angels ministered to him." In his struggles with Satan, Jesus was not alone.

We should ask ourselves: What temptations am I facing in my teaching right now? Who do I allow to minister to me?

Prayer

Jesus, sometimes I'm in a desert, too. Or at least I feel like I am. These are the times when I see little sense in what I do. I detect no life in it, no hope for the future. And I find myself saying, "What's the use?" I feel like giving up, or at least like making some cowardly compromises. That's when I know I'm engaged in real combat—with evil forces that threaten to arrest my enthusiasm, smother my hope, and put to death my love. Temptations are real, Jesus. I've experienced them.

But goodness is real, too. And (hopefully) goodness is even more real than evil—thanks to you. Be with me, Jesus, as I struggle against temptations in my personal and professional life. Come and minister to me during these trying times. Help me to see that the temptations I experience can serve to clarify my priorities, strengthen my resolve, and remind me of my absolute need for you. Amen.

---

4. Am I Called, Too?

Jesus said to them, "Come after me, and I will make you fish for people."   Mark 1:16–20

Reflection

No sooner had Jesus overcome temptation in the desert than he started to work. His first item of business was to recruit some helpers for his new venture.

There were many fishermen in Galilee in Jesus' time. Josephus the historian tells us that over 300 fishing boats sailed the waters of the sea of Galilee. It is to the shores of this lake that Jesus went in search of helpers. When we think about it, isn't that a little strange? Why didn't he go to the synagogue to recruit some learned rabbis? Why didn't he go to a more affluent neighborhood to seek the help of some influential men of means? Instead, Jesus went to the seashore, and this particular seashore was no French Riviera or Malibu. It was the working class district of his day: crowded, bustling, and (no doubt) pretty smelly!

And how did Jesus recruit his helpers? Not with a long speech presenting his theological beliefs. Not with promises of reward or threats of punishment. He recruited not by what he said, but by who he was. He won people over not with a multitude of words, but with his simplicity.

And who did he recruit? Common, ordinary, run-of-the-mill people—not unlike ourselves. From the beginning, the outstanding characteristic of the disciples of Jesus was their ordinariness. That should be a consolation for all of us who consider ourselves pretty ordinary individuals.

Mark describes two different callings in this passage: the calling of Simon and Andrew, and the calling of James and

John—two sets of brothers. The first call emphasizes the promptness of the disciples' response to Jesus' call. "Then they left their nets and followed him." There seems to have been no hesitation whatsoever.

The second call emphasizes the completeness of the response: they left their nets, their boat, and their father. In doing so, they walked away from their livelihood and, to a certain extent, even from their family. The actual work they would do is not clear yet. For the present, their preoccupation would be getting to know Jesus. (Not a bad preoccupation!)

This passage reminds us that Jesus was able to discern potential in individuals who appeared to be pretty ordinary. Do I see potential in the ordinary kids I teach?

Jesus continues to call people today. He speaks his "Come after me" even to me. Do I hesitate to follow him? If so, what holds me back?

Prayer

Jesus, call me! Let me hear those same words you addressed to those four fishermen on the shore of the sea of Galilee. Call me, Jesus, wherever you find me. Recruit me for the work of your mission. Win me over by the power of your presence.

And when I'm teaching, let me be more like you. Let me go where my students are. Let me touch them, not only by what I say, but also (and more importantly) by who I am. Give me eyes to spot potential in the ordinary kids who sit in front of me and help me to bring that potential to fruition.

Call me, Jesus. And I'll try to come—immediately and completely. Amen.

5. Jesus, You Wasted No Time!

On the sabbath he entered the synagogue and taught.
Mark 1:21–22

Reflection

Immediately after calling his first disciples on the shore of the sea of Galilee, Jesus headed for the synagogue in Capernaum. He wasted no time getting started with his work. The synagogue in Jesus' time was not only the place of worship, it was also the place where learned men took turns teaching the people. Mark tells us it was the sabbath, and he shows us Jesus taking his turn to teach.

Mark gives us few details here. All he says is that Jesus "entered the synagogue and taught."

"Taught what?" we want to ask. "Mark, you left out the most important thing: the content of Jesus' teaching!"

But not really. For the entire gospel of Mark, taken as a whole, gives us Jesus' teachings. We have only to meditate on it, passage by passage—as we're doing now—and gradually the content of Jesus' teaching will be revealed.

But here Mark limits himself to giving us a description of the congregation's reaction to Jesus' teaching: They were "astonished." Why? Mark tells us that, too. For Jesus "taught as one having authority and not as the scribes." And how did the scribes teach?

The scribes were the self-appointed "experts on the law." What they had done over the years was to break down broad religious laws or principles into literally hundreds of specific rules and regulations. They liked nothing more than to memorize these rules and teach them to the people—sometimes forgetting, unfortunately, what broad principle the specific rule was supporting. They were also fond of quoting authorities. In other words, they didn't come out and say what they believed or thought on a particular subject. Rather, they quoted what others had said and written about it. That was their focus, their methodology.

Mark says that the congregation was astonished by Jesus' teaching because it was so unlike that of the scribes. Perhaps this means that Jesus' teachings focused on broad religious principles and not on picayune regulations. And maybe it also means that Jesus risked sharing his own beliefs with the people rather than hiding behind those of some quotable authority.

In our efforts to teach as Jesus did, we might do well to ask ourselves questions about our own teaching methodologies. To what extent have I made Jesus' teachings my own? In my daily life, do I focus on broad principles or do I get distracted by lesser rules and regulations? Have I ever "astonished" anyone with my teaching? Have I ever astonished myself?

Prayer

Jesus, you wasted no time, did you? No sooner had you recruited a few followers than you set out for the synagogue to start your new ministry. Give me some of your resolution, Jesus, for I sometimes procrastinate (as you well know).

You entered the synagogue and began to teach the good news, and—by Mark's account—your first "lesson" was a huge success. For you taught in a way that "astonished." You focused on the "big picture" and didn't get lost in minutiae. You risked sharing your own thoughts and beliefs with your "class." And (as I well know) such sharing by a teacher is often fraught with risks. But, as you've shown throughout the gospels, and as I know from personal experience, the sharing of our thoughts and beliefs, often subtly, is what teaching is all about. It's the thing that ultimately astonishes.

Jesus, help me to see the big picture. And (while you're at it) give me a morsel of your daring, too. Amen.

6. About Unclean Spirits

Jesus rebuked him and said, "Quiet! Come out of him!"
Mark 1:23–28

Reflection

Someone once said, "You must get involved to have an impact. No one is impressed with the won-lost record of the referee."

In this passage Jesus "got involved" with an evil spirit. But this time the involvement didn't take place in some remote desert. It took place in the synagogue in Capernaum, where the evil spirit had taken up residence in a specific human being.

It was the evil spirit who initiated the encounter by crying out, "What have you to do with us, Jesus of Nazareth?" Notice that the spirit addressed Jesus by name. He knew who he was. He even referred to Jesus as "the Holy One of God." And the evil spirit also knew what Jesus' mission was all about: "Have you come to destroy us?"

Let's look at Jesus' response. Mark says, "Jesus rebuked him." That's a pretty strong verb. It means that Jesus reprimanded the spirit sharply. We can sense the anger Jesus felt when he shouted to the spirit, "Quiet!" The literal translation is "Be muzzled!" (How often are we tempted to shout that to one of our students!)

Then Jesus commanded the spirit to come out of the man. The unclean spirit did come out—but only after performing one final trauma on the man: "The unclean spirit convulsed him."

Once again the crowd was "amazed" at what Jesus had

done. They marveled that he had set forth "a new teaching with authority." Jesus' fame began to spread "everywhere throughout the whole region of Galilee."

There's much food for thought in this passage. First of all, Jesus was no wimp, he was no "pushover." It is clear that—when the occasion called for it—his "gentle love" sometimes took the form of indignation and even anger. This fact should console us when we confront "unclean spirits" in our work of teaching. Where might some of those spirits reside? Perhaps we encounter them in a selfish child or a mean teenager. Or maybe we meet them in an individual with a habit of lying, or a person with a flagrant disregard for the feelings of others. Or, we may even encounter unclean spirits in a parent who attempts to "bribe" us.

And, if we are honest, we know we encounter such spirits within ourselves as well—spirits of jealousy, greed, intolerance, despondency. How willing are we to engage in combat with such unclean spirits? Or, in the name of peace or even "gentle love," do we allow them free reign?

Prayer

Jesus, I've met unclean spirits, too. I've met them in the students I teach, in the atmosphere that sometimes permeates the school, and in others I have dealings with— from the administration to parents, from the school board to bus drivers to the local news media. And, if I'm really honest, I must confess that I meet unclean spirits in myself, too. Such spirits take many forms, but their general effect is the same: they disrupt, they afflict, they divide, they enervate. They are powerful forces to contend with.

Jesus of Nazareth, Holy One of God, cleanse me of my unclean spirits. Amen.

7. About Peter's Mother-in-Law

He approached, grasped her hand, and helped her up.
Mark 1:29–31

Reflection

After curing the man with the unclean spirit, Jesus went to Simon Peter's house. It's nice to know that Jesus made himself at home not only in the synagogue, but also in the home of a friend. When he arrived with his four disciples, Jesus was probably hungry and tired. (Teaching will do that to you!) Yet, things were not quite right in Peter's home. His mother-in-law was in bed with a fever.

The family immediately told Jesus about her. They seemed eager to share with Jesus their concern for the stricken woman. That tells us something important about Jesus: He was someone to confide in.

It's interesting to note that no one specifically asked Jesus to do anything about the ill woman. It was Jesus who took the initiative here. As Mark tells us, it was he who approached her—without being asked to do so.

Jesus grasped the woman's hand—another strong verb. And then he helped her up. Other translations say he "raised her up." (The word "raise" has definite resurrectional overtones.) At once the woman's fever left her. And what did she immediately proceed to do? She began to wait on her family and guests. We can imagine her saying, "Jesus, try my bread. I just baked it yesterday." And, "Simon, don't just sit there. See if anyone wants more wine."

There are other aspects of this story that make it enjoyable to think about. Notice how down to earth Jesus was;

how naturally he fit in here; how easily his disciples approached him with their concerns. And see the power of Jesus' touch. This is one cure he seemed to perform with very little effort. Also, note that Simon's mother-in-law had a fine understanding and appreciation of the gift of health. She used her newly restored health to be of service to others.

What can we learn from this simple vignette? To be attentive to others, to notice things: What mood are my students in today? Should I be concerned about altering their mood, or should I instead alter my plans for today? Who is "ill" today—a student, the principal, a teacher? Is there anything I can say or do to help them up, to lessen their fever? And, finally, how can I best use my gifts to serve others I meet today?

Prayer

Jesus, about Peter's mother-in-law . . . There are many jokes about mothers-in-law today, yet this woman, the most famous mother-in-law of the gospels, was anything but laughable. In fact, she comes across as immensely fortunate—first of all because she was touched and cured by you yourself! And second, she knew one of the secrets of happiness: serving others. How lucky can you get?

Jesus, invite me to share my troubles with you like Peter's family and your disciples did in this passage. Let me share the really big ones, as well as the small and seemingly petty. And when, like Peter's mother-in-law, I fall flat on my back, grasp me by the hand and bid me to get up and serve.

And help me to reach out and extend a helping hand to someone in need today: a student, another teacher, an administrator, a parent, whoever. Amen.

8. You Needed Time to Pray

"He got up and went out to a deserted place, and there he prayed." Mark: 1:35-39

Reflection

There's an old proverb that says, "If you are too busy to pray, you are too busy." That proverb could very well be the theme of this particular passage in Mark.

For, so far, Mark has shown that Jesus was very busy. He called some disciples, he preached and taught in the synagogue, and he cured one possessed man and one feverish woman (and quite a few others, too). The opening words of this passage present a sharp contrast to all this hubbub. They describe Jesus getting up before dawn and going off by himself to pray.

What a lesson is here for us! As busy as Jesus was, he still made time for prayer. As involved as he was with people, he still found time for quiet and solitude. Prayer seemed to be indispensable for him. It formed an integral part of his ministry.

If Jesus needed prayer, then how much more do we need it? If he couldn't carry on with his work without regular communication with God in prayer, then should we be surprised if we can't either?

Yet Jesus never used prayer as a technique for avoiding people. When the disciples finally found him, they told him, "Everyone's looking for you." We can probably empathize with Jesus here, for we too know those days when everyone's looking for us! And how did Jesus respond? He finished his prayer, came down from the mountain, and

18

plunged into his work again. Rather than feeling interrupted, he said to his disciples, "For this purpose have I come." Jesus had a real sense of mission.

And Jesus knew that prayer and ministry are meant, not to compete with, but to complement one another. Each can nourish the other; both are calls from God. My ministry of teaching should lead me to prayer, and my prayer should overflow into my ministry of teaching.

And so I ask myself: Do I bring the joys and concerns of my ministry to my prayer? Is my prayer life a source of encouragement and enlightenment for my teaching?

Prayer

Jesus, you needed to pray, too? That's good to know! It's good to know that you needed time to get away from it all. You needed time to be alone—time to pray. And you didn't wait to find time for prayer either. You made it. You carved out from your busy schedule definite periods for regular communion with God. Help me to do that, too. Help me to make time for prayer in my daily life. If you needed prayer, how much more do I need it!

But let not my prayer be an escape from reality. Never let me use prayer as a way of avoiding people or serious issues I should be facing. Help my prayer keep me honest. Help it to keep me enthused about my ministry.

And finally, Jesus, help me to see that both my prayer and my work are calls from God—both are holy. Amen.

9. What a Lucky Leper!

*A leper came to him (and kneeling down) begged him
and said, "If you wish, you can make me clean."*

Mark 1:40–42

Reflection

The disease of leprosy was fairly common in Jesus' time.
Considered highly contagious, it often disfigured its vic-
tims terribly. With no known cure, leprosy was the ultimate dread of the age—considered by many to be a fate
far worse than death.

It was little wonder then, that lepers were treated with
such harshness. Forced to dwell outside the city, usually in
caves, lepers were ordered to shout out loud warnings
whenever they ventured near the city. "Unclean! Unclean!"
they had to cry as a warning to passersby. Forbidden any
contact with others, lepers were the outcasts of Jesus' day.
They were the truly marginated, the "nobodies."

On this particular day, a leper approached Jesus. He was
daring. In full view of everyone, he fell down on his knees
and cried, "If you wish, you can make me clean."

It is interesting to note that the leper didn't actually ask
Jesus to cure him. He made a simple declarative statement—
implying that Jesus had the power to cure him if he wished to.

Perhaps the most important detail in the passage is when
Mark says that Jesus was "moved to pity." One translation
says "with anger," another says, "Feeling sorry for him. . . ."
Whatever the word choice, this fact is certain: Jesus reacted to the leper with deep emotion. He then did something that probably caused more than a few gasps among

his followers: He stretched out his hand and touched the leper. How courageous can you get?

The touch worked and instantly the leper was cured. Not only was his health restored, but so was his dignity and his fellowship with other human beings.

What does all of this have to do with education? On the literal level we can see some parallels. Despite our sophisticated medicine, we still have our dreaded diseases—from lice to AIDS. We can ask ourselves: What is our attitude toward anyone with any disease? Are we "moved with pity" as Jesus was or are we unconcerned? Or, worse yet, are we hostile? What kind of attitudes are we trying to instill into our students toward the sick?

On another level, we too have "lepers" in our midst. They sit in our classrooms; they stand alone on our playgrounds. They eat by themselves in our cafeterias and even in our faculty lounges. Have we tried to extend our hand to them?

Prayer

Jesus, what a lucky leper! He was lucky because he found you—someone capable of being moved with pity. Someone not afraid to express deep emotion. Someone courageous enough to reach out and touch an outcast, a nobody.

Jesus, help me to be more like you. Increase my sensitivity to the "outcasts" I encounter in my daily life. Give me courage to get emotionally involved in the lives of other people—my students, my fellow teachers, my fellow parishioners, the people in my local community.

And, Jesus, heal me of those things that separate me from others. Call me forth from the margins I sometimes retreat to. Reach out and touch me, for I know "if you wish, you can make me clean." Amen.

10. Talk About Ingenuity

It became known that he was at home. Many gathered together so that there was no longer room. . . .

Mark 2:1-5

Reflection

After preaching in the neighboring villages, Jesus came home to Capernaum. His fame had spread so quickly that crowds began to flock to hear him.

Mark paints a vivid scene here. Jesus was in the house preaching. So many people were crammed into the house to hear him that they overflowed into the street. From out of nowhere came four men carrying a friend on a stretcher. Although we know nothing about these men, we can make the following assumptions: They really cared for their sick friend; they possessed ingenuity; and they had strong faith in Jesus.

We can picture their disappointment when they got to the house only to find that it was jammed with people. There was no way they could even get near the door, let alone inside. The men had every right to be disheartened. Less resourceful men would have turned around and gone home, but they didn't. Instead, they came up with a very clever plan. The men carried their friend to the top of the house, ripped out part of the roof, and lowered the stretcher into the room below.

What a consternation that must have caused! Jesus stopped in the middle of his lesson plan. (He didn't have much choice!) And, turning his attention to the surprise new arrival, he said, "Child, your sins are forgiven." Why did he say this?

Mark gives us the reason: because "Jesus saw their faith." Whose faith? The faith of the paralytic—probably. The faith of his four friends—definitely.

This charming story reminds us how much our faith is linked to the faith of others. We might ask ourselves: From whom did I receive my faith? Who supports me in my faith now? And how do I encourage and support the faith of others—especially in my teaching?

Prayer

Jesus, talk about ingenuity . . . I really admire the ingenuity of those four men. I also admire their willingness to go out of their way for a friend. They were not deterred by a seemingly insurmountable barrier. They found a creative way to get around it (or more accurately, to go down through it) to achieve their goal. And how unselfish was their goal: the well-being of a friend in need.

Jesus, I ask for ingenuity, for resourcefulness. I ask for the knack to discover creative ways to get around (or over or under or through) the seemingly insurmountable barriers I encounter—in my classroom, in my school, in my personal life.

And finally, Jesus, I want to thank you for the faithful and "faith-full" friends you've put into my life—especially _____, _____, and _____. What would I do without them? Who would I be without them? Let me find ingenious ways to show them how much I appreciate them. Amen.

11. About Matthew

Once again he went out along the sea. . . . Mark 2:13–14

Reflection

Once again Jesus returned to the seashore. And once again he began to teach. It's amazing how the whole world seemed to be his classroom. And what a beautiful classroom it must have been with its blue vaulted ceiling, rhythmic beatings of the waves, and warming rays of the sun.

Jesus' teaching methodology was typical for rabbis of that time: He broke up his formal lessons with leisurely strolls with his students. These strolls were something like mini field trips. On one such stroll the group happened to pass a custom house, a tax-collecting place. Here Jesus saw a man named Levi (more commonly known as Matthew).

Mark tells us nothing about Matthew except that he was a tax collector, but we can read between the lines. First, we know that since Matthew was a tax collector, he was considered to be a Jew who had betrayed his race by working for the enemy, the Romans. Because of this, he was, no doubt, scorned and hated by other Jews.

Second, because he responded so quickly to Jesus' call, we can surmise that he had at least heard of—and maybe even seen—Jesus prior to this. Perhaps he had stood on the outskirts of the crowd and had listened to Jesus preach. (He would have had to stand on the outskirts, for the other Jews would not have allowed him to get much closer!)

Jesus said to him, "Follow me," and immediately Matthew got up and left his work. We can imagine the various reactions of the onlookers. There would be the shock among many of the Jews. We can almost hear them saying, "Matthew? You're inviting Matthew, Jesus? Don't you know what this guy does for a living?" Sure, Jesus knew—and yet he invited him anyway. Apparently Jesus saw more in this man than met the eye.

Then there would have been the reaction of the crowd to the deserted table with the stacks of money on it. Imagine the ruckus around that table when Matthew got up and walked away! Matthew displayed extraordinary generosity in doing this. He left a way of life—forever.

Jesus gives us much to reflect on in this passage: What is our teaching methodology like? Do we restrict our teaching to a specific room and formal lessons, or do we see opportunities for teaching everywhere? How good are we at seeing more in our students than meets the eye?

Prayer

Jesus, about Matthew . . . What an unlikely recruit! A traitor to Judaism! A worldly person! And yet you see potential in Matthew and invite him to be an apostle.

What consolation there is for me in Matthew's story. For at times I feel like an "unlikely recruit" for this ministry of education. Sometimes I feel unworthy, incompetent.

Be with me, Jesus. Reveal to me the goodness in myself that you see. Give me the courage to leave behind those things that distract me or actually pull me away from following you more closely.

And finally, Jesus, give me some of your insight into people. Help me to see more than meets the eye: goodness in the belligerent second grader, the sullen seventh grader, the cocky sophomore. And give me the wisdom and know-how to draw that goodness forth. Amen.

12. The Company You Kept

"Why does he eat with tax collectors and sinners!"

Mark 2:15-17

Reflection

The old proverb says, "We are judged by the company we keep." In this passage, we see that the scribes and Pharisees did just that: They judged Jesus by the company he kept.

Prior to this, Jesus extended an invitation to Matthew to become one of his followers. It was then Matthew's turn to extend an invitation, and he invited Jesus to come to his house for a meal. Jesus accepted readily, and his disciples came with him. Mark tells us that there were other guests—"many tax collectors and sinners"—who were also at the table. We shouldn't be surprised. Matthew's occupation had ostracized him from the community. Therefore, Matthew the "outcast" invited other outcasts of the community to dine with him.

And Jesus sat in their midst, evidently enjoying himself. Of course, some of the scribes and Pharisees were shocked to see the company Jesus was keeping. They brought their complaint not to Jesus himself, but to his disciples. "Why does [Jesus] eat with tax collectors and sinners?" they asked.

Jesus overheard their question and defended his behavior with a simple metaphor: "Those who are well do not need a physician, but the sick do." He was implying that the "sick" were the so-called "sinners." Lacking health or wholeness, these were precisely the people who needed Jesus, the "physician," the most. And in the long run, these "sinners" would prove themselves far wiser than the scribes and Pharisees, for they knew they needed healing, and thus, they welcomed Jesus into their lives.

What is impressive in this story is how at home Jesus was with all kinds of people—even the outcasts from the community. His metaphor about the physician is an apt one for us and our ministry of education. We might ask ourselves who gets *our* attention. The "healthy" students or those who are "sick"? Do we find ourselves favoring the attractive ones, or do we give ourselves also to the unattractive?

Jesus was under the scrutiny of the scribes and Pharisees, who watched his every move. Too cowardly to confront him directly, they confronted his disciples. But Jesus nipped that behavior in the bud. When they wouldn't confront him, he confronted them.

Sometimes we, too, are under scrutiny as educators. And sometimes we, too, must not be afraid to defend our actions. Jesus did.

Prayer

Jesus, look at the company you kept: sinners and tax collectors! They certainly weren't attractive people to be with. Who likes to keep company with outcasts? And yet you did—you saw their need for you.

In my teaching, there are some students I'd rather not keep company with: the ornery, the slow, the dull, the immature. And yet, these are the students who probably need me the most. Give me strength and patience to be with them, to work with them—even when they don't invite me.

And, Jesus, come into my "house"—my heart, my family, my classroom. Sit at my table and eat my bread. Talk to me; listen to me; share your insights with me. Let me never forget that I am a sinner who needs your healing touch. Amen.

13. About Feasting and Fasting

The disciples of John and of the Pharisees were accustomed to fast. Mark 2:18-20

Reflection

This passage focuses our attention on two basic rhythms in life: fasting and feasting.

Mark tells us that the disciples of John the Baptist and the Pharisees were both accustomed to fasting. Although in the Jewish religion there was only one compulsory day in the year to fast, the Day of Atonement, the stricter Jews chose to fast twice a week: Mondays and Thursdays.

What are some reasons we might choose to fast? For one thing, fasting is a form of self-discipline. By denying ourselves legitimate pleasures such as foods we enjoy, we prove that such things do not control us. Rather, we control them. Fasting is also a wonderful way to appreciate things. Doing without something helps us not to take it for granted. Fasting might also be done out of love for someone—love for God or for another person.

Certainly Jesus was not against this type of fasting. He objected to fasting to get attention or to demonstrate piousness. Those types of fasting were merely "for show."

In this passage, Jesus also made reference to fasting's complement—feasting. The followers of Judaism knew how to feast. For example, the celebration of a Jewish wedding didn't last a mere day—it lasted a full week!

Jesus used the image of the wedding feast to say something important about his mission. He compared himself to the "bridegroom" at a wedding feast. By doing so, Jesus was clearly saying that the spirit of his mission was to be characterized primarily by feasting— by joy, by celebration. Since, by our teaching, we share in the mission of Jesus, shouldn't joy be the characteristic spirit of everything we do?

For we certainly have cause for rejoicing. After all, we have Jesus! He continues to be with us today—in the Eucharist, in scripture, in loving relationships, in compassionate service of others. Shouldn't our faith and our ministry, then, have the aura of joy?

As teachers, we try to convey this great truth to our students—that Christian faith is essentially one of joy. We must help them to see that being good has its own rewards, that doing the right thing can give considerable pleasure, and that helping others can bring much happiness. The best way to do this is to practice what we preach—being a joy-filled Christian.

Prayer

Jesus, I know about fasting and feasting. For both are connected with my ministry of teaching. I fast every day—from laziness, selfishness, impatience, sullenness, and crabbiness. I fast as a way of showing my love for you and for the people you've put into my life—especially my students.

But, I feast every day, too. I feast on insights gained in prayer, a little child's spunk, a bigger child's creativity, a teenager's show of concern, a fellow teacher's sense of humor.

Thank you for helping me to see how both fasting and feasting play a role in my life and ministry. Help me to appreciate more and more your active presence in my life.

And finally, Jesus, help me to be more of a "party person." I ask this through the power of your joy-filled Spirit. Amen.

14. New Wine, Fresh Wineskins

"No one sews a piece of unshrunken cloth on an old cloth."   Mark 2:21-22

Reflection

In this passage, Jesus used two highly effective images to convey an important truth. How did he come up with these images? He certainly didn't pull them out of a hat or find them in an encyclopedia. Most likely, he extracted these images from his own experience.

I imagine he got the first one from his mother, Mary. The Holy Family were essentially poor folk. If clothes got ripped, they didn't just throw them away and buy new ones. If clothes were worn, they didn't put them in a bag and donate them to the St. Vincent de Paul Society. No, they mended and patched them—they made them last.

If Jesus was a typical little boy (and there's no reason to think he wasn't), he probably was good at tearing his clothes—by falling down on rocks, by climbing over fences, by running through prickers. And when he got home, Mary probably scolded Jesus and ordered him to take off the torn clothes so that later that day she could patch them for him. I imagine that, after watching his mother mend his clothes many times, Jesus learned that, "No one sews a piece of unshrunken cloth on an old cloak."

The wineskin image he probably got from Joseph. As a young boy he would have helped his father make wine. Maybe one day when they had just finished making some new wine, Jesus poured it into an old wineskin. Suddenly the wineskin burst and all the new wine went splattering all over the place. After Joseph had helped Jesus clean up all the wine and his anger had subsided, he probably said, "Remember, Jesus. New wine, fresh wineskins!" And Jesus might have thought to himself, "New wine, fresh wineskins. I like that! Someday I'll use it!"

Prayer

Jesus, new wine, fresh wineskins—I like that, too! I think it's wonderful the way you employed concrete images to convey religious truths. And how your images were based on your experiences—like mending clothes and making wine.

Jesus, help me to teach that way. Help me to teach not solely from books, or from my head, or from what others say, but also (and more importantly) from my own experience. Give me the creativity to use effective images—especially those that will speak to my students.

And give me a love for the new. Give me the courage to try new things. Make me willing to discard pet methods, favorite techniques, and old lesson plans that no longer work with the students sitting in front of me. I ask this from you—who came to make all things new. Amen.

15. About the Sabbath

They watched him closely to see if he would cure him on the sabbath so that they might accuse him.

Mark: 3:1–6

Reflection

Have you ever felt you were being watched? Have you ever felt everything you did was being scrutinized and judged? Jesus did. As he was teaching once again in the synagogue, the Pharisees—the religious leaders—were sitting in the back of his classroom taking notes. Not a very comfortable situation for Jesus to be in. And yet, he carried on with his lesson with incredible calm.

When he spotted the student (the man) with the withered hand, Jesus was moved to act. He didn't have to. He could have pretended he didn't notice the man's deformity. (We humans are sometimes good at ignoring people who need help.) Or he could have whispered to the man, "See me after class, and I'll see what I can do about that hand of yours," thus avoiding any conflict with the religious authorities. But no, Jesus invited the man up to the front of the classroom, where the man became a kind of walking-talking audio-visual aid.

Jesus' question to the Pharisees is an important one. "Is it lawful to do good on the sabbath?" he asked. By asking this, Jesus put this particular cure within a much broader context: the very meaning of the sabbath observance. He showed the Pharisees that they had reduced the sabbath observance to ritual. He reminded them that observing the sabbath has little to do with legalistic practices, but everything to do with compassionate responses to those in need.

Jesus showed two strong emotions in this passage. He had pity for the deformed man and anger toward the Pharisees. In front of everyone, he bid the man stretch out his hand, and instantly the hand was healed. What an excellent demonstration lesson! Restoring the man's hand was more than a cosmetic healing. The withered hand, no doubt, made it difficult or even impossible for the man to make a living. By restoring the hand, Jesus enabled the man to earn a living once again. The healed hand is a symbol of new life.

This fact makes the last sentence even more ironic: "The Pharisees went out and immediately took counsel with the Herodians against him to put him to death." Jesus' powerful lesson on the meaning of the sabbath could cost him his life.

Prayer

Jesus, about the sabbath . . . You were not against "keeping the sabbath." You just differed with the Pharisees on how it should be "kept." They kept it by adhering to a multitude of rules and regulations. You kept it by adhering to one law: love God and others.

Jesus, help me to examine the rules and regulations that govern my life, especially the ones I make up for myself— make others happy, mind your own business, try to be perfect, work hard. Give me the honesty to articulate these rules and the wisdom to evaluate them from time to time in terms of love.

And help me to evaluate the rules in our school and in my teaching place—the written ones and (maybe even more importantly) the unwritten ones. May all the rules I formulate and all the rules I keep serve only this: your great law of love. Amen.

16. You Were Good with Crowds

A large number of people followed from Galilee and from Judea. Mark 3:7–10

Reflection

In a few of the previous passages, we saw the growing hostility of the religious authorities toward Jesus. They were watching his every move in an effort to gather evidence to use against him. At one point they made the decision to eventually "put him to death." In this passage we find a sharp contrast to their animosity—the crowds of common folk loved Jesus! They enthusiastically flocked to Jesus to see him, to hear him, to touch him. They couldn't seem to get enough of him.

Mark shows that Jesus' popularity was growing geographically as well. No longer was his fame restricted to Judea, it had spread to outlying areas such as Jerusalem, Idumea, Tyre, and Sidon. The crowds here consist of real people from real places. What's more, Tyre and Sidon were foreign territories. The implication is that even the gentiles were beginning to come to Jesus.

The scene was wild, hectic, and excited. So numerous were the people and so eager were they to touch Jesus, that he feared being crushed by them. He told his disciples to have a boat handy, just in case he had to make a quick getaway.

There are probably a number of aspects of this story that we can identify with. Just as we have probably encountered some hostility on occasion, we have also probably experienced periods of popularity. These are the days when we feel as Jesus did in this passage. Everyone wants us. (Or everyone wants a piece of us!) The principal asks to see us, the school secretary requests a "little favor," another teacher asks for help, a parent calls, and the janitor stops in to see us about a work order we wrote three months ago.

And then there are our students—they're after us, too! They're begging for our attention; they're tugging at our sleeve; they're asking us a million questions—all urgent and all at once. And we suddenly realize, that unlike Jesus, we have no boat handy into which we can escape.

Whoever said being needed was easy? Whoever said being popular was fun? Sure, on some days it does feel good to be needed. It's a real morale booster to feel popular. But on other days, it's not easy at all. We feel trapped, pulled apart, and even taken advantage of.

On those days, we should to look to Jesus. He understands whatever we are experiencing in our teaching—whether it be hostility, popularity, or something in between.

Prayer

Jesus, you were good with crowds. People came from all over to see you, to hear you, and to touch you. They came to be cured of their diseases and to be cleansed of their unclean spirits. They were real people, from real places, with real problems and real hopes. Very much like me—and the people I minister to and with.

Jesus, give me energy to make myself available to serve others. After all, that's what the word minister means: to serve. And sometimes serving entails being pushed and shoved and pressed upon.

And, Jesus, teach me to handle well both hostility and popularity. Don't let either one of them get in my way of loving you and the individuals you have put into my life. Amen.

17. Please Mission Me!

*He appointed twelve (whom he also named apostles)
that they might be with him. . . .* Mark 3:13-19

Reflection

In this passage, Jesus took some of his followers up to a
mountain. It is there that he appointed his twelve apostles.
In addition, he gave the twelve men two important assignments. The first was to "be with him," and the second was
"to go forth." It's interesting to note that the phrase "to be
with him" actually means the same thing as the word "discipleship." That should remind us that all Christian discipleship starts with being with Jesus. But it doesn't end
there. Discipleship also entails a going forth "to preach"
and "to drive out demons." We go forth with both our
words and with our good deeds.

What Jesus did made a lot of sense. He was gaining in
popularity and drawing large crowds, and he realized the
limitations of his person set against the immensity of his
mission. He knew there was no way he could reach everyone. He was already thinking about the future, too. Jesus
needed his apostles not only to help him with his mission
in the present, but also to extend his mission into the future.

Jesus chose those twelve as his first "recruits." He then
transformed their minds and hearts with his person and his
teaching and sent them forth to minister to the people.

Much of this passage consists in a listing of the names of
the twelve apostles. The names remind us that Jesus chose
specific individuals with varied family backgrounds and
life experiences. To put it bluntly, the twelve apostles were
a motley group. Among them were several fishermen, a tax

collector, and even a religious fanatic. Their temperaments also varied—from the hot-headed to the cool, from the talkative to the taciturn, and from the overbearing to the shy. In fact, these men had little in common—except their love for Jesus. That's what drew them together in the first place, what united them.

What does this passage teach us about our ministry of education? First, it reminds us that we are missioned to do what we do. Our ministry wasn't our idea; it wasn't our choosing. We might have felt extremely drawn to it, or we might have been reluctant to teach. Whichever the case, the fact still remains: We are missioned to do what we do. The invitation and the power come from Jesus.

Second, we bring our whole selves to our ministry. Like the apostles, we bring our individuality—with our specific backgrounds, temperaments, talents, likes and dislikes, and teaching styles. As a Christian community it is our diversity that enriches us and our love for that Jesus unites us.

Prayer

Jesus, please mission me! Mission me as you missioned your first twelve apostles. Call me to come to you, to be with you. In the privacy of my room, in the quiet of a church, in the solitude of a short stroll, in the seclusion of a bath or shower. Call me—everyday.

Then send me forth. Send me forth to teach your message of love, to cast out the demons of ignorance, violence, apathy, hatred, and greed.

And Jesus, may the diversity in our school community be our source of enrichment. May our love for you be our source of unity. Amen.

18. You Are the Sower in My Life

In the course of his instruction he said to them, "Hear this!"
                                                              Mark 4:1–9

Reflection

Once again we see that Jesus employed imagery to get his point across—imagery familiar to his "students." Since this particular lesson was given outdoors, it's not too farfetched to imagine that Jesus might have seen a sower out in some distant field. His, "Hear this!" is sometimes translated as, "Listen! Look!" Perhaps he directed the people's attention to the man and then proceeded to make his analogy.

Once again, this story illustrates Jesus' incorporation of everyday happenings into his religious teachings. He seemed to see no clear distinction between the secular and the divine and was keenly aware of how much the everyday world is infused with the holy.

Jesus was always aware of his listeners' frame of reference, their point of view. In this case, he knew that the people around him were familiar with growing crops. He entered their frame of reference in order to share with them the broadness of his own point of view. This wonderful technique is the basis of all good teaching.

Jesus did another pedagogically sound thing in this passage: He made the abstract concrete and the complex simple. The word of God became the seed and the various levels of receptivity of different people were the different soils. It's an analogy that still works today, but what does it mean?

In the few verses that follow, Jesus explained his analogy: There are many different ways to respond to Jesus, to the Word of God. Some individuals seem incapable of accepting him, of receiving him into their hearts at all. Others accept Jesus—but only for a while. Their enthusiasm soon wanes and their faith dries up. Some people's faith sprouts up, but it is choked by the thorns of life. But then there are those who fully welcome Jesus into their hearts and produce a "hundredfold."

The image of the sower is an apt one for what we do in the classroom. We sow seeds, but don't necessarily reap fruit. Our students possess different degrees of receptivity. We can do things to try to clear the land and enrich "their soil," but sometimes, despite all our effort, the seed will not take root. Can we live with this reality? It's the reality Jesus lived with.

Prayer

Jesus, you are the sower in my life. Help me to make the soil of my heart more receptive to your word. Uproot the thorns that tend to choke your word—the thorns of despair, laziness, selfishness, pride. Give me the deep roots of patience, compassion, and an abiding sense of humor.

And, Jesus, help me to sow your word in the students you have given me to teach this year. Enable me to appreciate their frame of reference, their point of view, so that I might more effectively share with them my own—and yours.

And finally, in my teaching please give me the gift to make the abstract concrete and the complex simple. Amen.

19. About the Lamp of Faith

He said to them, "Is a lamp brought in to be placed under a bushel basket...?"　　　　　Mark 4:21–25

Reflection

This passage from Mark contains four distinct sayings of Jesus. Even though they're grouped together here, there's no reason for us to try to see some connection between them. Instead, let's look at each one individually and try to figure out its meaning.

The first—one of Jesus' most popular sayings—is that no sensible person hides a lamp under a bushel basket or under a bed. The purpose of a lamp is to shine, to give light. What could the lamp represent in this extremely short parable? Most people believe that it represents faith.

What Jesus meant, then, is that we should not hide our Christian faith away somewhere—it should be seen. The faith we profess should be expressed in how we live our lives and in our teaching.

The second saying is about truth: "There is nothing hidden except to be made visible; nothing secret except to come to light." It seems as if Jesus was saying that ultimately truth will triumph. How consoling this is for those of us who work so hard to pass on the "truth"—whether it be expressed in a mathematical formula, a religious creed, or a Shakespearean sonnet—to the next generation.

The third saying is: "The measure with which you measure will be measured out to you." In other words, "What you give is what you get." As teachers, we know this well. If we want respect from our students, we must respect them. If we want them to trust us, we must first trust them. There is a direct correlation between giving and receiving, between loving and being loved.

And finally, the fourth saying deals with the incomprehensibility of God's ways at times. Jesus said, "To the one who has, more will be given. From the one who has not, even what he has will be taken away." We might object, "That's not fair!" But the saying reminds us that God's ways are not always our ways. We must ask ourselves to what extent can we live with the mystery of God's ways in our own lives, while helping our students to do the same.

Prayer

Jesus, I thank you for the lamp of faith—the precious gift you've given me. Make it shine brightly for all to see. And I thank you for the gift of truth. Give me a greater appreciation of its beauty and worth. Help me to teach the truth by everything I say and do.

Jesus, what I give is what I get. Help me to be a more generous giver—especially to the people you've put into my daily life.

And, because God's ways are not always my ways, help me to trust God more and more. Help me to also encourage in others—especially my students—a greater trust in God. Amen.

20. The Lesson on Growth

Of its own accord the land yields fruit, first the blade, then the ear, then the full grain in the ear....

Mark 4:26–29

Reflection

Every time we pray the Our Father we say the words, "Thy Kingdom come." This short parable by Jesus, found only in the gospel of Mark, tells us how the kingdom of God comes.

Jesus compared the coming of the kingdom to the growing of crops. He began by describing the work of a typical farmer. The farmer plants the seed and, although he watches over it and cares for it, he doesn't actually make the seed sprout and grow. When it comes to growing crops, the farmer is more observer than cause, more bystander than catalyst. The miracle of growth lies within the seed itself and is affected by other factors over which the farmer has little if any control: sun, rain, and temperature.

Something similar occurs in our teaching. Although we can watch over our students and care for them, there's precious little we can do to actually cause them to grow. So much depends on the students themselves, as well as other factors over which we have little control: family background, biological makeup, parental involvement, societal pressures, and so forth. As teachers, sometimes we feel more observer than cause, more bystander than catalyst. Such a realization can be a little humbling. Are we able to accept the very real limitations involved in the teaching-learning process?

In this parable Jesus said something else about how the kingdom of God comes—it comes gradually: "First the blade, then the ear, then the full grain." Similarly, we teachers know that education is a gradual process. Sometimes the growth in our students is discernible and can even be measured. But most of the time it isn't. Can we live with that reality and continue to teach day after day, even when we see little or no growth?

And finally, in this parable Jesus spoke with certainty of the final harvest: "And when the grain is ripe, he wields the sickle at once, for the harvest has come." The kingdom of God is coming—despite our limitations, despite appearances to the contrary, despite apparent setbacks. The kingdom of God is coming—we have Jesus' word on it!

Prayer

Jesus, teach me again the lesson on growth; teach me again the lesson of its mystery; teach me to reverence life tucked away in seeds and (much more importantly) in people. Remind me that inactive is not the same as lifeless, that dormant is not the same as dead, that inert is not the same as hopeless.

Give me the humility to accept my limitations as a teacher and to work creatively with the many other factors that influence (for better or for worse) the growth of my students.

But most of all, Jesus, give me a deep realization of the certainty of the final harvest. Let my daily prayer be, "Thy kingdom come! Thy kingdom come!" Amen.

21. The Mustard Seed

"It is like a mustard seed that, when it is sown in the ground, it springs up and becomes the largest of plants. . . ."   Mark 4:30–32

Reflection

This parable of the mustard seed has always been a favorite of mine. It goes back to my sophomore year in high school, when I studied the life of Christ. I had an exceptionally fine teacher that year, Sister Karla Bognar, SND, who was always coming up with creative assignments for us kids. For one such assignment, she asked each of us to take one of the parables of Jesus and present it to the class in an effective way. I got stuck with the parable of the mustard seed. I remember thinking, "It's so short! How can I make this parable come alive for the class?"

At home that night I went to the kitchen and opened the drawer where my mother kept the spices. Sure enough, I found a box of mustard seeds. Opening it, I was struck by how tiny they were. How could I best convey their smallness? I did two things in class the next day.

First, I passed a mustard seed down every row so the other kids could actually hold one in their hands and experience its smallness. Then I got out a quarter and began putting mustards seeds on it very carefully—counting aloud as I did so. To everyone's amazement I could fit about 25 mustard seeds on one quarter. Now that's pretty small!

In Jesus' time, the mustard seed was a common symbol for smallness. When Jesus likened it to the kingdom of God, he was saying something more than, "Good things come in small packages." He was saying, "Marvelous, incredible, magnificent, and grand things often begin small."

To what extent have we bought into this teaching of Jesus? Or to what extent have we bought into our contemporary culture's teachings: Numbers determine everything, value is measured solely by magnitude, big is better, the only thing that matters is the bottom line?

Sometimes as teachers we get discouraged by smallness. We ourselves feel small—the proverbial "voice crying out in the wilderness." Or we're tempted to think, "I'm only one person. What good can I do?" Or "I have these kids for so short a time. What impact can I realistically expect to have on them?" We may even get disheartened by our students—by their small numbers, by their apparent lack of interest, or by their ordinariness.

It's times like these that we should remember the tiny mustard seed. Maybe we should even tape one to our desk as a visual reminder—small is good, the ordinary is beautiful, the seemingly insignificant is packed with promise.

Prayer

Jesus, often I feel as small and insignificant as a lowly mustard seed. But your parable reminds me that true worth goes far beyond size and numbers.

Jesus, help me to accept the "smallness" of what I do in the ministry of teaching. Give me the courage to believe in the coming of your kingdom, even when there is little visible evidence. And finally, renew my conviction that, through little me, you can accomplish mighty things. Amen.

22. I'm Afraid of Storms

A violent squall came up and waves were breaking over the boat. . . .   Mark 4:35–41

Reflection

The sea of Galilee was known for its sudden storms, which could arise with little or no warning. In this passage Jesus got into a boat with some of his disciples and started to cross the sea. Mark tells us that a "violent squall" came up and "waves were breaking over the boat." And what was Jesus doing during this terrible storm? He was sleeping "on a cushion" in the rear of the boat!

The disciples were "terrified." Since these men were very familiar with sailing this body of water, we can surmise that this particular storm must have been exceptionally fierce. They awoke Jesus and cried, "Teacher, don't you care that we're perishing?"

Their cry is sometimes our cry, too. It is the cry of one of our deepest fears—that nobody, not even God, cares about what is happening to us.

Jesus answered this cry with quick and decisive action. He rebuked the wind and told the sea to be quiet and "be still." These are the same words that Jesus used earlier, when he drove the demon out of the possessed man. Instantly "the wind ceased and there was great calm."

But that is not the end of the story. The most important part is still to come: Jesus then asked his disciples, "Why are you terrified? Do you not yet have faith?" He was implying that faith has the power to cast out fear. If we trust in Jesus, we will not be terrified, even if storms are raging around us.

This passage can be misleading. Its point is not that Jesus will make all our storms go away—that would be unrealistic and even unhealthy—but that adversities, though difficult, can be good for us. The great educator, Mother Janet Stuart, said, "We are not at our best when we are most exuberant, most enthusiastic, most eager, but when we are pulling most gravely, steadily, courageously in our appointed duties, when we are almost swamped by difficulties, weariness, seeming impossibilities, but all the time our face bravely turned toward Eternity, our heart lovingly toward God."

Prayer

Jesus, I'm afraid of storms. Like your disciples, I'm terrified of the storms raging around me—the violence I see on our streets, in our homes, and in our schools. And I'm also afraid of the storms inside of me—the fears I have that I'm not giving my students what they really need to face this turbulent world.

And so, Jesus, I bring my fears to you. I lay them at your feet and wait for your response. It's quick in coming. I hear you say to me, "Why are you afraid? Don't you yet have faith?"

Increase my faith in you, Jesus. Help me to see adversity not solely as a foe, but also as a friend. Help me to realize that I'm not at my best only when I'm most enthusiastic and eager, but also when I'm working steadily and courageously in my appointed duties—with my heart turned lovingly toward God. Amen.

23. Mr. Jairus Was a Great Dad

*Jesus said to the synagogue official, "Do not be afraid;
just have faith."*   Mark 5:21–24, 35–36

Reflection

The passage about the raising of the daughter of Jairus has special significance for teachers. For, like Jesus, we often have to deal with anxious parents.

Jairus, we are told, was "one of the synagogue officials." That means he was one of the chief administrators of the local synagogue, a man with considerable authority.

We've seen Jesus dealing with religious authorities prior to this encounter. And, sadly, most of those dealings were not very friendly. But Jairus was different from the other religious leaders. He came not to challenge Jesus, but to beg his help.

The meeting between Jesus and Jairus is significant. Both men had good reason to be suspicious of one another. But instead, both men put aside their mistrust. Jairus, who was absolutely desperate, humbly asked Jesus to come heal his daughter, who was "at the point of death." And Jesus, who was absolutely generous, readily agreed to do so and followed Jairus to his home.

But before they even got to the house, they were met by people from Jairus' house who brought him the sad news: "Your daughter has died." These same people concluded, "There's no use for Jesus to trouble himself any longer."

It was obvious that Jairus had faith in Jesus' power as long as his daughter still had life in her. Now he was being asked to have faith in Jesus even though his little girl was dead. The lesson seems to be that no situation is ever totally hopeless, as long as Jesus is involved.

Jesus turned to Jairus and said, "Don't be afraid. Just have faith." These words are the same words he spoke to his disciples in that storm-tossed boat. Jairus must have found faith somewhere in his heart, for both he and Jesus continued their journey to Jairus' home.

Jesus' treatment of Jairus can be used as a model for the way we treat the parents of our students—even if some of them come to us with considerably less humility and docility than Jairus did! We must meet them with trust in our hearts, speak to them with respect, and put aside any prejudices we might have. And we must believe that they do love their child—even if their love is sometimes shown in ways we can't fully understand or agree with.

Prayer

Jesus, Mr. Jairus was a great dad, wasn't he? He was totally consumed with the well-being of his little girl. He went to you himself, threw himself down at your feet, and begged you to come and cure her. What anguish must have been in his heart!

And you were so quick to respond to his pain. You didn't look upon Jairus as "one of them." No, you saw him as an individual with a specific request.

Jesus, help me to lay aside my prejudices in my dealings with others—especially my students and their parents. Make me more aware of the times I stereotype others with words such as these: "Those fourth graders!" Or "What can you expect from freshmen?!" Or "That Mrs. So-and-So is such a pain!" Or "All janitors are alike!" Help me to see and relate to people as individuals who are uniquely loved by you. Amen.

24. Becky Jairus Was a Lucky Kid

"Little girl, I say to you, arise!" The girl, a child of twelve, arose immediately and walked around. . . .

Mark 5:37–43

Reflection

When Jesus arrived at Jairus' house, he let only three of his disciples accompany him inside: Peter, James, and John. It was these same three disciples who would also be with him at the Transfiguration and in Gethsemane. They were something like Jesus' "inner circle."

At the house they were met with a "commotion." The professional mourners, family, and friends were "weeping and wailing loudly." Their expressions of grief called attention to the poignancy of the situation: A young girl had died before reaching womanhood. Such a thing is truly a cause for great weeping.

But Jesus told the mourners, "The child is not dead but asleep." And they laughed him to scorn. "Who is this jerk?" they might have asked among themselves. For professional mourners such as these surely knew death when they saw it.

Then Jesus took charge once again. He put the mourners out—which probably did not please them—and, taking Mr. and Mrs. Jairus and the three disciples with him, he entered the room where the little girl lay. Jesus took her by the hand and said to her in her language of Aramaic, "Little girl, get up!" She got up immediately and walked around.

Everyone in the room was "utterly astounded." Jesus' final directive was a touching one. He told the girl's family to give her something to eat. After all, she was not a ghost—ghosts don't eat. She was a real, living, and now healthy, little girl—and real, living, healthy little girls eat!

Jesus' behavior here is a good model for us as teachers. Notice how calmly he faced ridicule and how quickly he took decisive action. Notice, too, that Jesus took the little girl by the hand—connected with her. And he spoke the language of the little girl (and her parents). And finally, how solicitous he was for the little girl's total well being.

Prayer

Jesus, Becky Jairus was a lucky kid! (I don't know if that was her name or not, but what difference does it make?) She had a caring family, and she had you! What more could she have needed?

And how beautiful you were in this passage. You faced commotion with calm and ridicule with dignity. Amidst hopelessness and death you brought hope and new life. While others stood around utterly astounded, you remembered the small details—like a little girl's hunger.

Jesus, take my hand like you took the hand of Jairus' daughter. Speak to me your words of calm, hopefulness, and new life, and help me to do the same for others. Direct my attention to the agitated, the mournful, the hungry, and let me "utterly astound" them with the good news of your love. Amen.

25. Let Me Touch Your Cloak

She said, "If I but touch his clothes, I shall be cured."
Mark 5:25–34

Reflection

Tucked inside the story of the raising of Jairus' daughter to life, is the story of the woman with the hemorrhage. Her condition was certainly a pitiful one, for she had suffered from her affliction (probably some sort of severe uterine bleeding) for twelve long years. Mark also tells us that she had turned to the doctors of her day and had "spent all that she had," and still her condition was not helped. In fact, it "only grew worse."

The woman's condition was no doubt physically enervating and psychologically embarrassing. It also had religious ramifications. According to the book of Leviticus, the bleeding rendered the woman ritually unclean. This meant she was cut off from the worship of God and from the fellowship of her local community.

In her desperation, she turned to Jesus. The nature of her affliction made a public request for healing too difficult for her. Instead, she decided that by secretly touching only his clothes, she would be healed—so strong was her belief in Jesus' power,

The woman's plan was successful, but the story doesn't end there. The instant the woman was cured, Jesus was aware that power had "gone out from him." He began asking who it was that had touched him in such a faith-filled way.

The woman eventually stepped forward in "fear and trembling," and fell at Jesus' feet, telling him "the whole truth." Jesus addressed her as "daughter," thus indicating that she was a member of the family of God. Then, in front of everyone, he praised her for her great faith, which made the miraculous healing possible.

What a strong and courageous woman she was. She didn't sit around bemoaning her affliction. She took positive action and went to Jesus. Her cure wasn't the result of some magical power that flowed from Jesus' clothes. It was a direct result of her deep faith in the power of Jesus.

Do I take my afflictions to Jesus—no matter how embarrassing they may be for me? How strong is my faith these days?

Prayer

Jesus, let me touch your cloak. For you are sensitive enough to feel it. There you were, being pressed on from all sides, being pushed and shoved by the crowds, and yet you detected this one woman's particular touch—a touch of faith. Give me that same kind of sensitivity to detect the faith in the individuals who crowd into my life.

Jesus, give me some of this woman's humility—to turn to you with all my worries and concerns, as well as my joys and accomplishments. Give me some of this woman's spunk. Help me to take positive action and try to heal the afflictions that beset the greater world, as well as my own personal world.

And finally, Jesus, let me hear you speak to me today those words you spoke to her: "Your faith has saved you. Go in peace." Amen.

26. You Can't Go Home Again

He was amazed at their lack of faith.   Mark 6:1–6

Reflection

Two proverbs come to mind when we read this passage from Mark. First, "Familiarity breeds contempt." And second, "Beauty is in the eye of the beholder."

Jesus returned to Nazareth, his home town, with his disciples and went to the synagogue on the sabbath to teach publicly. The people were "astonished" when they heard him. "Where did this man get all this?" they asked each other. "What wisdom he displays, what mighty deeds he performs!" Yet their astonishment did not lead them to faith, it led them to cynicism. "Who does this guy think he is?" they ended up saying.

The problem with the home town folks was that they thought they knew who Jesus was. And on one level they did. They'd seen him as a carpenter—a working person like themselves. They knew his family. In short, their familiarity with Jesus blinded them to the fact that he could be anything else but a common, ordinary human being. "He can't be great. We know him, and he's too much like us," they concluded.

"Beauty is in the eye of the beholder." How we perceive reality depends on what's inside of us. The true tragedy for the people of Nazareth was two-fold. By failing to allow Jesus to be anything more than what he used to be, they missed out on realizing who he really was. And, by failing to perceive the greatness in ordinary people, they failed to realize the greatness even in themselves.

We must not make the same mistake as the people of Nazareth. Do we allow people—our students, their parents, other teachers and administrators—to be more than we think they are? What is our understanding of the "ordinary" in daily life? Do we pass over it, or do we appreciate its beauty and greatness?

Someone has defined a cynic as a person who knows the price of everything but the value of nothing. Cynicism in a teacher is deadly. But faith, which enables us to see the true value of everything, is life-giving.

Prayer

Jesus, you can't go home again. You tried to go back home to Nazareth, and look what happened. What should have been a wonderful experience, turned out to be a terrible disappointment. After a successful "road tour," you probably expected to be greeted with enthusiasm and faith in your own home town. But instead, you are met with cynicism and disbelief.

Jesus, give me a greater appreciation of the familiar, the ordinary: the school or parish in which I teach, the lessons I try to convey, the students sitting in front of me, the other people with whom I minister. Let me see their goodness and beauty. Let me never take them for granted or hinder their growth with my low expectations.

And, Jesus, I welcome you into my life. Continue to astonish me with your teachings and your love for me. Amen.

27. Taking Nothing for the Journey

He summoned the Twelve and began to send them out two by two. . . .　　　　　　　　Mark 6:7–13

Reflection

In this passage Mark describes in vivid detail the missioning of the apostles. Let's focus on several of those details to see what insights they might give us into our own ministry of education.

First, it was Jesus who commissioned the twelve. It was he who sent them forth to teach. The same is true of us. We teach not simply because we want to or because the school or parish is desperate for a teacher. Being mindful of this fact can provide us with courage, enthusiasm, and a deep trust in the one who sends us forth.

Jesus sent the apostles out "two by two." This fact should remind us that we can't do it alone. If the first apostles needed one another's support and companionship, then don't we?

Jesus instructed the apostles "to take nothing for the journey but a walking stick." Perhaps this directive is telling us that we can't let things tie us down. Perhaps it is telling us that we must not put our trust in things; instead, we must trust in God to provide us along the way with what we need to teach.

What kind of things tie us down as teachers? We can get tied down to a lesson plan—so much so that we become inflexible. We can get tied down to a schedule, a definite way of doing things, a certain grade level, or a particular group of kids. But Jesus seemed to say, "Don't get tied down. Pick up your walking stick and move on."

As teachers, we can also begin to trust in the wrong things. We can trust in our past experience, our audio-visual aids, our way of maintaining discipline. Although some of these aspects of teaching are important, they are unworthy of our deeper trust—only God is worthy of that.

Jesus told the apostles, "Whatever place does not welcome you or listen to you, leave there and shake the dust off your feet in testimony against them." As teachers, we won't reach every student. We must try, of course, but with some students there might come a point when we will have to give up, admit defeat, and move on. Are we able to entrust such students to God's love when our own efforts have apparently failed?

Prayer

Jesus, about taking nothing for the journey . . . Your directives here are difficult. It's difficult for me to let go and move on. It's difficult for me to let go of a student I cannot reach. It's hard for me to admit defeat.

But your directives here are also wise, Jesus. You sent your disciples "two by two." Help me to draw support from those with whom I minister, and let me be a source of encouragement for them. Give me eyes to see those things that can tie me down as I teach, as well as those things that can set me free.

But, most importantly, Jesus, make me realize anew that I am sent forth by you. Give me a deep, strong sense of your presence in whatever I do. Amen.

28. I Come and I Go

His heart was moved with pity for them, for they were like sheep without a shepherd. . . . Mark: 6:30–34

Reflection

What image comes to mind when we think of the word "teacher"? What analogy would we use to describe what we do when we teach? Do we think of ourselves as a parent, coach, doctor, entertainer, gardener? The image we have of ourselves as teacher reveals a lot about what we think we're really doing in the classroom.

In this passage Jesus gives us a unique image for teachers. We find it in the last line: "His heart was moved with pity for them, for they were like sheep without a shepherd and he began to teach them many things." The analogy is that a teacher is like a shepherd. Let's explore this comparison.

What is the primary role of a shepherd? First, the shepherd guards the sheep from life-threatening dangers. Don't we do something similar in our teaching? Aren't we trying to protect our students from the life-threatening dangers to which they are exposed every day—dangers such as ignorance, low self-esteem, injustice, violence, poverty, despair?

Second, the shepherd leads the sheep to green pastures, to nourishment. We, too, attempt to lead our students to things that will provide nourishment for them on their journey through life—to the green pastures of faith, truth, beauty, goodness, and love.

And finally, the shepherd provides the sheep with a sense of security, with the feeling that they are being cared for because they are of value. Do our students sense how much we really care for them? Do we give them a sense of security by our steady presence in their lives day after day? Do we convey to them how valuable they are in our eyes and, by extension, in God's eyes?

Mark tells us that Jesus was "moved to pity" for the people. Once again Jesus reacted with deep emotion. His teaching arose not out of a sense of duty or a desire to impress or control others—it arose out of his deep sense of compassion. What's my motivation for teaching?

Prayer

Jesus, I come and I go. Like you. Like your disciples, who you called to come aside and rest a while. Make me sensitive to those times you do the same for me. Tell me to come. Invite me to rest a while. And give me the courage and the wisdom to do so.

And, Jesus, when it's time for me to become engaged again in the lives of other people, tell me to go. And give me the courage and energy to do so. Help me to be a true shepherd to the children you've given to me to teach—to guard them, to provide them with nourishment, and to express my deep love for them. May all my teaching, like yours, proceed from love and compassion.

And finally, Jesus, be my shepherd-teacher. Lead me, nourish me, and love me. Amen.

29. I Have Only a Few Loaves

Taking the five loaves and the two fish and looking up to heaven, he said the blessing. . . . Mark 6:35—44

Reflection

We can probably readily identify with the apostles in this story of the multiplication of the loaves and fishes. Jesus was teaching and—so eager were his students to learn from him and so intriguing was Jesus' lesson—he went way beyond the dismissal bell. It was "already late," and the apostles suddenly realized that the people needed to be fed. They informed Jesus of this fact and then offered him a suggestion: Send the people away.

If we're honest, we sometimes do the same thing when we perceive a need that we assume is far beyond our resources to do anything about. It can be a global need, like world hunger. Or it can be a local need: a student with special needs. Like the apostles, we might be tempted to say, "Let someone else deal with this problem. Who am I to think I can possibly have an impact? My resources are so meager!"

Jesus responded to the apostles' suggestion with this question: "How many loaves do you have?" In other words, he was directing the apostles to look to themselves for a possible solution to the peoples' need for food. The apostles might have been indignant at Jesus' question, yet they did as he said and began counting bread and fish. They came up with a scant five barley loaves and two fish. They (as we are) were keenly aware of the meagerness of their resources and the apparent hopelessness of the situation.

But Jesus told the people to sit down. He took the food

the apostles had provided, he blessed it, and he directed the apostles to distribute it. Incredibly, there was enough food to go around. All the people ate and were "satisfied." And what's more, they had twelve baskets of leftovers!

One lesson comes shining through in this story: We are to give not merely out of our surplus; we are to give even out of our need. We are to offer what little we may have to others. And, through Jesus' hands, our little is made great.

Prayer

Jesus, I have only a couple of loaves. In that way, I'm a lot like your apostles. I'm sometimes overwhelmed by the needs I see all around me—in my school, my parish, my local community, my country, my world. And like the apostles, I'm tempted to plead with you, "Please send these people (and these problems) away!"

But let me hear those same words you spoke to your apostles: "How many loaves do you have?" And let me realistically take inventory of my gifts and talents—no matter how meager they may seem. And let me willingly and generously put them into your hands.

Then dazzle me with the wonders you can work—even through the likes of me! Show me again and again the marvels you're able to work with meager assets and limited funds.

And finally, Jesus, give me a renewed appreciation of the gift of the Eucharist, which this beautiful story foreshadows. Invite me to come regularly to your table to be nourished with the Bread of Life. Amen.

30. Make the Winds Die Down

He went off to the mountain to pray. . . .   Mark 6:45–52

Reflection

There are three sentences in this gospel passage that merit our reflection. The first one is, "He went off to the mountain to pray." Once again, Jesus felt the deep need for communion with God despite his hectic schedule. What might have been the content of his prayer? Perhaps he was thanking God for the success of his preaching. We could ask ourselves, do we thank God for the successes we experience in our teaching? Both the major ones (a certain ornery student is becoming more cooperative) and the minor ones (Scott remembered his homework today).

Or perhaps Jesus was praying about his apostles, for the last few lines of the passage are significant. Mark says that the apostles "had not understood the incident of the loaves." In other words, they had missed the point of the miracle—an exceptionally fine demonstration lesson, to say the least! Perhaps Jesus was a little weary of his "prize pupils" and was talking with God about them. Do we talk to God about our students on a regular basis? Do we ask for God's help to reach our students?

Another sentence that is striking in this passage is this: "But when they saw him walking on the sea, they thought it was a ghost and cried out." The apostles recognized Jesus, but they didn't think he was real. Consequently, they were terrified. We say we believe in Jesus, but how real is he for us? How involved is Jesus in our personal lives? How well do we incarnate his teachings—and thus make him real—in all that we do? Perhaps the level of our fear is the measure of our lack of faith in the real Jesus.

The third sentence that is highly significant is, "He got into the boat with them and the wind died down." Jesus is in the same boat with me—no matter what I may be experiencing in my teaching. If I'm energized and happy, Jesus is there to share that with me. If I'm weary and disheartened, Jesus is with me, too. Aware of his presence, I suddenly realize the winds are beginning to die down.

Prayer

Jesus, come to me across the waters. . . . You knew your need for prayer, your need for regular communion with God. Help me to appreciate my need for continual prayer.

Jesus, your apostles didn't understand the multiplication of the loaves. They didn't get the message. Be patient with me when I, like them, miss the point. And give me the strength to be patient with my students when they fail to grasp what I'm teaching.

Jesus, come to me across the waters that surge around me. Help me to relate to the real you and not to some ghost of my own fabrication. Climb into my boat with me and make the winds die down. Or, if that's not immediately possible, then at least give me a sense of your very real presence alongside me in my rocky boat. For just knowing that you are really with me is enough to take my fears away. Amen.

31. About That Deaf Man

Immediately the man's ears were opened . . . and he spoke plainly. Mark 7:31–37

Reflection

Here we have another healing story. Mark tells us that this one took place in "the district of Decapolis." That means it occurred in a predominantly gentile area. This fact reminds us that Jesus had come to serve not only his own people, but also the gentile peoples. His love was not confined to one nation; it was directed toward all nations.

Mark tells us that a group of people brought the deaf man to Jesus. They were his emissaries, for the man himself was unable to speak. Jesus took the man off by himself— "away from the crowd." This is an intriguing detail. What could it mean? Perhaps it means that Jesus wanted some privacy to work this cure. Or, as someone has remarked, it might show that Jesus didn't treat this particular man as a "case"; rather, he treated him as an individual.

Jesus' methods for healing in this story were the same methods that other healers used in his day. He put his fingers in the man's ears and touched spittle to the man's tongue. Both touch and spittle were commonly thought to have healing powers. Then Jesus looked up to heaven, thus acknowledging that his power came from God. He groaned deeply—as if this particular cure was costing him something. He said in Aramaic, "Ephphatha!" and immediately the man's ears were opened and he could speak.

The people were "exceedingly astonished" at what Jesus had done, and they said, "He has done all things well. He makes the deaf to hear and [the] mute to speak." These words are a direct paraphrasing of the words of the prophet Isaiah (35:5–6), as he described Israel's final deliverance. By putting them here, Mark is saying, "Israel's time of deliverance is at hand. For Jesus is here!"

We can learn much from Jesus in this short narrative. His love had no bounds. Does mine? He treated people not as cases or clients, but as individuals. Do I? His ministry of healing cost him something. Does my ministry of teaching cost me anything? And Jesus didn't let popularity go to his head. Do I?

Prayer

Jesus, about that deaf man . . . He reminds me of the gifts I tend to take for granted: the gifts of hearing, sight, speech, smell, taste, touch, mobility. Give me a greater appreciation of all the gifts I have and a greater sensitivity to those who are physically or emotionally challenged.

Jesus, increase my ability to relate to people as individuals—especially my students. Let me never treat them like mere cases or clients. Increase my willingness to pay the cost involved in serving others—the cost of sleepless nights, worry and concern, discouragement, uncertainty, and fatigue. And help me to pay this cost cheerfully.

And finally, Jesus, open my eyes to the many rewards involved in serving others out of love for you. And all that you to do for me, may I do for others. Amen.

32. I'm Like That Blind Man

Then he laid hands on his eyes a second time. . . .

Mark 8:22-25

Reflection

One of Mark's favorite themes in his gospel is the theme of sight and blindness. This passage, which falls almost in the middle of his gospel, reiterates this theme. On one level it tells the story of Jesus' cure of a single blind man. On a deeper level it describes the blindness of many people—especially the religious leaders—to who Jesus was. It also underscores the point that even Jesus' closest followers, his disciples, did not yet have a clear vision of who he really was.

The passage is similar to others we have already read. Once again a group of friends brought an ill person to Jesus. This anonymous "they" begged Jesus to "touch him." Notice there is no mention of faith in this cure as there was in most of the other healings. Jesus put spittle on the man's eyes, laid his hands on him and asked, "Do you see anything?" The man, who was beginning to regain some of his sight replied, "I see people looking like trees and walking." Jesus laid his hands on the man a second time and the man fully regained his sight.

Why with this healing did it take Jesus two tries to cure the man? Perhaps it was meant to be symbolic of the difficulty of Jesus' struggle to cure the "blindness" of the religious leaders and his own disciples. Or maybe the gradual cure was meant to point out that most healings occur in just that way—gradually.

What immediately follows this story is Peter's profession of faith. As strong as that profession appears to be, it was nonetheless short-sighted—as we shall see.

The story of the cure of the blind man reminds us that we all are "blind" to a greater or lesser degree. How blind am I to Jesus' presence in my everyday life—especially in the people I live and work with day after day? How effective am I at sharing the Christian vision of life with my students?

The curing of this blindness happens gradually. Am I able to accept the fact that most growth is a gradual process, or do I get impatient for quick results?

Prayer

Jesus, I'm a lot like that blind man. Sometimes my sight is blurry. I find myself groping in the dark. I'm undiscerning and unperceiving. I fail to see your subtle or even blinding presence in my daily life.

Take me by the hand, Jesus. Lead me from places where darkness rules. Lay your hands upon my eyes and give me new sight. Let me not become impatient when vision seems to come slowly; rather, help me to be satisfied (and even happy) with gradual growth—in myself, my loved ones, my colleagues, my students.

I ask you these things through the power of your enlightening Spirit. Amen.

33. Jesus, Who Are You?

Along the way he asked his disciples, "Who do people say that I am?"   Mark 8:27–30

Reflection

So far in Mark's gospel, Jesus had been doing quite a bit of teaching. And, as we have seen, his teaching got him into considerable trouble with the religious leaders of his day. But, like any good teacher, Jesus knew it was time to find out to what extent his primary students, namely his disciples, had grasped the important lessons he had taught them. So he decided to give a test, an oral test. And a short one, for it consisted of only two questions.

Jesus asked his disciples an easy first question: "Who do people say that I am?" All that the disciples had to do to get this one right was to report back to Jesus what other people had been saying about him. Easy enough. And the disciples handled this question well. They told Jesus something like, "Well, Jesus, 30 percent say you're John the Baptist, 28 percent say your're Elijah, 20 percent say you're one of the prophets, and the rest are undecided."

Jesus must have nodded his approval at such a fine answer, and the disciples must have smiled and patted each other on the back for their response. But then Jesus asked the second question, the hard one, the only one that really counted: "Who do you say that I am?"

The disciples were probably taken aback by this one. "Who me?" they might have each asked in disbelief. And Jesus probably nodded and smiled, "Yes, you. Each of you." I imagine there was a rather long pause before anyone dared to answer this question. But then Peter, not known for his timidity, finally attempted an answer. He said to Jesus, "You are the Messiah."

Peter gave the proverbial "right answer": the Messiah. But, as we shall see shortly, his understanding of the concept of Messiah was grossly incomplete. He chose the correct word, but he certainly didn't have a clear understanding of the meaning of that word.

We aren't much different from Peter, are we? We, too, get lucky and use the right words at times—Jesus, love, faith, education, community, prayer. But our understanding of the real meaning of these words is sometimes extremely limited or even way off base. Perhaps we should ask ourselves on a regular basis the meaning of such key words in our lives. And perhaps we should pray that their meaning may become more clear to us as we continue our journey through life.

Prayer

Jesus, who are you? It's easy for me to tell people who others think you are, but it is very difficult for me to tell others who I think you are. Help me to realize that the only thing that really matters in my life is my answer to your question: "Who do you say that I am?" And I give that answer not only in what I say or teach about you, but also in how I live my life.

And, Jesus, just as I take regular stock of my students' comprehension of my lessons, remind me to take regular stock of my own comprehension of key words in my life: love, faith, education. I ask this of you because I completely agree with Peter's answer to your question: "You are the Messiah." Amen.

34. I Shy Away from Suffering

He began to teach them that the Son of Man must suf-
fer greatly . . . and rise after three days.   Mark: 8:31–33

Reflection

In the passage prior to this one, Peter declared that Jesus was the Messiah. He gave the right answer to Jesus' question, but, as this passage illustrates, Peter had a lot to learn about what the word "Messiah" really means.

Mark begins this passage with these words: Jesus "began to teach them." Why the word "began?" Jesus had been teaching the disciples all along. But now his teaching was taking a new direction—that he, the Messiah, "must suffer greatly and be rejected . . . and be killed . . . and rise after three days." What could that have possibly meant to the disciples? By their reaction, they seemed to dwell on the suffering and death part of Jesus' lesson. How shocked they must have been. How incomprehensible his words must have seemed to them.

It is no wonder then, that Peter reacted so strongly to Jesus' words. Mark tells us he took Jesus aside and "rebuked" him. This indicates just how strongly opposed Peter was to what Jesus had proposed. And Jesus reacted strongly to Peter, as well. He rebuked Peter—even calling him "Satan."

What did Jesus mean when he called his apostle "Satan"? He probably meant that Peter's way of thinking— to avoid suffering and death—was in line with Satan's way of thinking. There might be a hint here that Jesus himself had been struggling with Satan, who was trying to convince him to play it safe and avoid suffering and death at all costs.

Jesus then told his disciples, "You are thinking not as God does, but as human beings do." These words are vital ones for all of us who claim to be Christian. The history of the church gives ample examples of the thinking of human beings being in opposition to God's thinking—for example, the condoning of slavery, the violent persecution of "non-believers," injustices toward women.

What about my own personal history? Have there been times when my thinking has been opposed to God's thinking? And what about my ministry of education? Would God approve of the way I teach my classes, or do I always play it safe and avoid "suffering and death" at all costs?

Prayer

Jesus, I shy away from suffering. That's why I can completely sympathize with Peter's reaction to this teaching of yours. What do you mean you're going to suffer greatly, be rejected, be killed? It's too much to take! At least that's the way I look at it.

And that's just the problem, isn't it, Jesus? I tend to look at things only from my point of view and not from God's. That's the point you were trying to get across to your disciples. And that's the point you're trying to get across to me, too, isn't it?

Jesus, broaden my perspective. Help me to see a place even for suffering and death in my life. Give me the courage to face the particular sufferings that accompany my ministry of teaching. May my thinking be more and more in accord with the thinking of God—and your thinking. Amen.

35. About Hard-to-Take Words

"Whoever wishes to come after me must deny himself, take up his cross, and follow me."　　　　Mark 8:34–38

Reflection

What are some of the maxims of our age that many people live by? "Watch out for number one!" "Do all you have to do to make it to the top." "Your worth is determined by how much money you make." "Success is living in a certain neighborhood, driving a certain car, belonging to a certain country club." "Avoid pain and inconvenience at all costs!"

It is good to keep these in mind as we reflect on Jesus' words in this passage, for then we will realize just how radical his teachings really were. Jesus had a way of reversing things, of turning things inside out. And if we want to be numbered among his followers, then we might first have to have our world turned upside down.

Our contemporary culture says, "Me first!" Jesus says, "Deny yourself." He taught that we should think more about others than ourselves, devote our energy and resources to helping others, be ready to sacrifice for love of them, and be willing to put ourselves second if need be, or even last. In short, Jesus believed that we should focus more on giving than getting.

Our modern world says that suffering is evil and should be avoided at all costs. Just look at the number of ads for pain killers! But Jesus said, "Take up your cross." He was totally honest with his disciples. He was not inviting them to discipleship under false pretenses; he was telling it like it was. Our culture emphasizes profit, the proverbial "bottom line." But Jesus asked, "What profit is there for people to gain the whole world and forfeit their lives?" The ultimate value is life, and the only bottom line is the amount of love with which we live it.

The words of Jesus contradict so much of what our world holds in esteem; his values reverse the values our culture espouses. Some might say, "He was too idealistic!" or, "What he was asking for is well nigh impossible!" But the key phrase in the entire passage is, "Follow me." These words remind us that we're not merely espousing philosophical or theological principles—we're loving a person, Jesus. And that person was not merely expostulating a pet theory, he was describing the way he actually lived.

Prayer

Jesus, your words are hard to take. I don't like to be reminded of the fact that pain and suffering go hand-in-hand with following you. And I'm sometimes uncomfortable with trying to uphold Christian values that are largely at odds with the values of the society in which I live.

Jesus, help me to follow you more closely and to remember that you never ask of me what you yourself have not faced. And, what's even better, you walk with me! Continue to be with me as I feebly try to deny myself, take up my cross, and follow you. Amen.

36. About Your Transfiguration

And he was transfigured before them, and his clothes became dazzling white. . . .   Mark 9:2-8

Reflection

Immediately prior to the event described in this passage, Jesus had shared with his disciples the sober prediction of his passion and death. He then took three of his disciples to a mountain top with him and there he was "transfigured before them." Some scripture scholars see this event merely as some sort of dazzling display Jesus put on to encourage his despondent apostles. But surely there was more to it than that.

The aura of light that surrounded Jesus might represent some sort of interior illumination he experienced at this moment—a profound realization of who he was and what his mission would ultimately entail. Notice that here, like at Jesus' baptism, the affirming voice of God was heard: "This is my beloved Son." But this time, the words were not in second person. They were not addressed to Jesus; rather, they were in the third person—as if directed to the three disciples. The implication is that Jesus already knew he was God's beloved, but the disciples needed to be reminded of this fact, especially since they were about to see him arrested and put to death.

Mark tells us that the three apostles with Jesus were Peter, James, and John. These were the same three who witnessed the raising to life of Jairus' young daughter. They were the three who would also accompany him to the garden of Gethsemane. What was their reaction to what happens here? They were "terrified," Mark tells us. They were speechless—except for Peter who blurted out, "Rabbi, it is good that we are here!" Peter knew a peak experience when he saw it! Then he offered a suggestion—"Let us make three tents: one for you, one for Moses, one for Elijah."

Peter had "missed the boat" again. He saw the transfiguration as some sort of event that canceled out Jesus' predictions of suffering and death. It was almost as if he was saying, "Let's stay here forever! Let's forget about that suffering! Let's enjoy this ecstasy forever!" Whereas Jesus would have said, "Yes, let's enjoy this ecstatic moment, but let's remember its purpose: It is meant to confirm me in my resolve to do the Father's will—which entails suffering and death. Enjoy the mountain top ecstasy, but remember we must go down and walk in the dark valley below. But God's love is there, too."

The transfiguration is an event that every Christian disciple must undergo—again and again. Like Jesus, we will have times when things are going well for us and we have a deep sense of God's love. We will taste sweet success and feel competent, accepted, and successful. But sooner or later, we will experience those dark valleys. Perhaps we will experience significant failure, the limitations of aging or ill health, gross confusion or uncertainty. And maybe we will have little or no sense of God's love. Hopefully at such times we will be challenged to live our faith on a deeper level, to trust, even in the darkness, the illuminating power of God's faithful love.

Prayer

Jesus, about your transfiguration . . . I readily identify with Peter here. I, too, would want this good time, this "high" to last forever. For that's how I feel about the highs in my own life.

So I begin this short prayer by saying thank you, Jesus. Thank you for the many good times I've known, the many peak experiences I've had in my life: a small achievement, a relationship that nourishes, a time when I felt a profound sense of God's personal love for me. These highs encourage me and sustain me in my resolve to do the Father's will.

But thank you for the "valley" days, too. For the hard times I've known, the "lows" I've experienced: a small failure, a relationship that debilitates, a time when I felt totally abandoned by God. These lows call me to greater faith and love.

Help me to see both the highs and lows as part of God's will for me. And remind me that God's love is with me always—on a mountain top, in a deep valley, or somewhere in between. Amen.

37. What Faith and Prayer Can Do

"Teacher, I have brought to you my son possessed by a mute spirit."   Mark 9:14-29

Reflection

Jesus and three of his disciples—Peter, James, and John—had just come down from the mountain where Jesus had been transfigured, and immediately they ran into a crisis. A man had brought his possessed son to Jesus' disciples, and they had been unsuccessful in their attempts to rid the boy of his demon. Jesus quickly took charge. He asked the father, "What seems to be the problem here?" And the father described the pathetic condition of his son.

As teachers, we can well empathize with Jesus here. How many times have we walked into the middle of a crisis? And how many times have we listened to the sad stories of parents pleading with us to help their child?

Jesus' response to the man was one of frustration: "O faithless generation . . . how long will I endure you?" Yet he didn't allow his frustration to impede his work. "Bring the boy to me," he said. Then, before curing the boy, Jesus reminded the father that "Everything is possible to one who has faith." The man replied, "I do believe, help my unbelief!"

The description of the healing is reminiscent of other healings that Jesus had performed. Mark says, "Jesus took him by the hand, raised him up, and he stood up." These words have definite overtones of resurrection.

Once alone with Jesus, his disciples asked him why they were powerless to drive out the demon. Jesus' reply is significant: "This kind can only come out through prayer."

Some of our students are "possessed by evil spirits"—the spirits of low self-esteem, greed, envy, anger, ignorance, and the like. Their parents plead with us to heal them. And we try. Sometimes our efforts are rewarded with visible success. Other times we appear to fail. But whatever the outcome may be, our method must be accompanied by faith and prayer. Those are the two essentials of the methodology of a follower of Jesus.

Prayer

Jesus, faith and prayer can drive out demons. That was the lesson of this passage. In one dramatic exorcism you taught the absolute necessity of faith and prayer. Say to me those same words you spoke to the father of that boy: "Everything is possible to one who has faith." And hear my response: "I do believe, help my unbelief!" For, although I have faith in you, I realize how imperfect that faith really is.

And again, Jesus, give me a greater appreciation of the role of prayer in my ministry. Help me to pray for my students—that they may be rid of the evil spirits that sometimes torment them. And help me to work more closely with their parents to free them from whatever holds them in bondage.

I ask these things of you through the power of your resurrection. Amen.

38. How Am I Doing?

They had been discussing among themselves on the way who was the greatest.   Mark 9:33-37

Reflection

Someone once said, "Those who travel the high road of humility are not troubled by heavy traffic." As we see in this gospel passage, even Jesus' very own disciples could sometimes be anything but humble. Jesus was on his way to Jerusalem to suffer and die and they were taken up with arguing about which of them was the greatest.

Jesus didn't let the incident pass. Like a good teacher, he asked them, "What were you doing back there?" Although he probably knew what they were doing, he gave them an opportunity to explain their behavior to him. They did—probably with considerable embarrassment. Jesus used the embarrassing incident to teach a wonderful lesson.

He began by stating the concept he wished to get across: "If anyone wishes to be first, he shall be the last of all and the servant of all." Next he employed a highly effective audio-visual aid to reinforce that concept: He set a little child in their midst. (It's interesting to note that the Aramaic word for child is "talya"—which is also the word for "servant.") And, "putting his arms around" the child, Jesus said to the Twelve, "Whoever receives one such child as this in my name, receives me; and whoever receives me, receives not me but the One who sent me."

Perhaps we teachers should have these words written across every lesson plan we teach from as a daily reminder of what we are actually doing when we teach: We are receiving children in Jesus' name. And when we do this, we are receiving not only Jesus himself, but also the One who sent him. We have Jesus' word on that!

In this short passage, Jesus spoke volumes. He clarified the essence of Christian discipleship—discipleship is service. True greatness in the Christian community is not found in rank. It is not found in other things we sometimes use to determine worth: titles, roles, salaries, educational degrees, age, gender. True greatness, according to Jesus, is found only in loving service.

The "high road of humility" is seldom congested. But with Jesus' help, it can become slightly more trafficked.

Prayer

Jesus, how am I doing? That's a question I ask you often. For, like your disciples, I worry about how I'm doing— compared with others. I worry about how I'm "ranked" with them. Am I a better teacher than so-and-so?

Jesus, it's embarrassing for me to admit these worries. Remind me that the one thing necessary is to serve others with love. And let me remember that such service can take many different forms. Give me a keen appreciation of the ways I already serve others and the ways I can do still more. And help me find creative ways to encourage an attitude of loving service in others—especially my students.

And finally, Jesus, let me, like that little child, feel your arms around me so that I may appreciate anew my own tremendous value and worth. Amen.

39. There's a John in Me

John said to him, "Teacher, we saw someone driving out demons in your name, and we tried to prevent him because he does not follow us." Mark 9:38–41

Reflection

In this passage the apostle John went to Jesus with a complaint: The disciples had seen a man who was not a disciple driving out demons in Jesus' name. They tried to stop him, because "he does not follow us." But what really bothered the disciples was that the exorcism apparently worked!

Let's look at some of the factors at play here. Although we don't know for sure the interior feelings and motivations of John, we can take a few intelligent guesses. First, John, and we can assume the other disciples, had lost track of the goal of their mission. They didn't rejoice that a person had been cleansed of a demon; they were upset that someone outside their circle had performed the exorcism. Do we sometimes lose sight of the goals of our mission of teaching? Do we get hung up on other factors?

Second, the apostles seem to have been jealous. They were overly protective of something they had every right to prize: their special relationship with Jesus. They resented the fact that an "outsider" was using Jesus' name to work wonders and wanted Jesus to do something about it.

Jesus' response to the situation was quite a contrast to that of his disciples. Instead of getting upset, he said, "Don't try to stop the man." Then he explained, "No one who performs a mighty deed in my name . . . can at the same time speak ill of me." Jesus wasn't threatened by someone using his name. He was impressed by the man's deed—a successful exorcism that brought relief to a tormented individual. Then Jesus said something that demonstrated just how tolerant he really was: "Whoever is not against us is for us." The disciples wanted to wall people out; Jesus wanted to welcome people in. The disciples tended to be "exclusive"; Jesus was all-inclusive.

Jesus concluded by gently reminding his fretful disciples that even the smallest act of kindness in Jesus' name—the giving of a cup of water—will be rewarded by God. What good news that is for us teachers, for so much of our teaching is composed of small kindnesses: smiling at a child, listening to a teenager, talking with a parent, doing a favor for another teacher, encouraging an administrator.

John went to Jesus with a complaint. Jesus used that complaint as a springboard, to teach his disciples a magnificent lesson on the importance of tolerance and acts of kindness.

Prayer

Jesus, there's a John in me. That's both good news and bad news. The good news is that I value my relationship with you. I'm proud to be "in your circle." I'm happy to work wonders in your name. But the bad news is that I am sometimes jealous of others, and feel threatened by the good they do. I know I'm guilty of this when I set myself up as being better than everyone else; or, when I put myself down as being worse than everyone else.

Jesus, exorcise me of the demons of jealousy and intolerance. Help me to feel secure in your love for me. Give me an expansive heart that welcomes other people into my life and world. And inspire me to keep performing those many small acts of kindness in your name. Amen.

40. I Love Kids, Too!

"Let the children come to me; do not prevent them, for the kingdom of God belongs to such as these."

Mark 10:13-16

Reflection

If ever there was a scripture passage for teachers, it's this one! What Jesus did in this story, we do every day by our ministry: We welcome little children into our lives.

This incident takes on greater significance when we put it into context. Jesus was on his way to Jerusalem to suffer and to die, and yet he had presence of mind and time enough to stop and play with little children. He had time to hug them, converse with them, and bless them. The incident shows just how much children must have meant to Jesus. How much they mean to us, too, who devote so much of our time and energy to educating them.

Jesus' warmth with the children was in direct contrast to his disciples' coldness. They tried to shoo the mothers and children away. "The Master is too busy!" they might have said. "He's got more important things to do!" How little had the disciples incorporated Jesus' values into their own lives.

Let us not forget the mothers. In Jesus' day, it was not unusual for Jewish mothers to bring their children to a noted rabbi for a blessing. The fact that the mothers chose Jesus bespoke the esteem they had for him.

And let us not forget the kids. The fact that the children went to Jesus so willingly attested to Jesus' approachability.

Jesus said, "The kingdom of God belongs to such as

these"—the children. What qualities do children possess that make them likely candidates for God's kingdom? For one thing, they're vulnerable and impressionable. They're open for change. Children are also humble, often keenly aware of their limitations. They tend to be trusting—especially of adults. And most kids have an innate sense of wonder that marvels at everything from a shag carpet to a yellow dandelion.

As teachers, we must never forget that we're learners, too. Our students can teach us many things—like what it means to be childlike. And by doing so, they can help to make us worthy candidates for the kingdom of God.

Prayer

Jesus, I love kids, too! Why else would I have become a teacher? I love their simplicity, their enthusiasm, their vitality, their laughter. I love being a witness to their growth, and I'm happy and proud when I can play a small part in encouraging or facilitating such growth in them.

Jesus, I'm glad you liked kids. It doesn't surprise me, for you had such a great sense of values! You found time to be with children even as you were facing the terrible personal tragedy of your arrest, torture, and death. Share with me your ability to be truly present to others even in the midst of personal worries and concerns.

Jesus, I love kids. Why else would I have become a teacher? Thank you for calling me to such a wonderful work! It prepares me well for the kingdom of God! Amen.

41. Anything Else?

"Good Teacher, what must I do to inherit eternal life?"
Mark 10:17–22

Reflection

The exchange between Jesus and that nameless man was an intriguing one. Notice how bold the man seems to have been. He ran up to Jesus, knelt down before him, and addressed him as "Good Teacher." Jesus was not taken in by the flattering title. He reminded the man that the adjective "good" was normally reserved to describe God.

The man's question appears to have been a sincere one: "What must I do to inherit eternal life?" His question was a sign that he was not fully satisfied with how he was living his life. Jesus gave the man a typical answer. He told him to keep the commandments—and even listed some of them so that there was no mistaking what he meant.

The man replied that he had done all of those things but was still not satisfied. Then there is that beautiful line: "Jesus, looking at him, loved him." Mark is saying that Jesus was somehow really attracted to this individual. There was something about the guy that Jesus really liked.

That's good for us to know, for we, too, are naturally more drawn to some individuals than to others. Take our students, for example. There are some students we probably like the first time we meet them—that we are naturally more attracted to than others. It's consoling to know that Jesus experienced these same feelings.

Then Jesus told the man what he still needed to do: "Go sell what you have, and give it to the poor . . . and follow me."

We would like the story to have a happy ending. We'd like the man to have said, "Sure! I'll do just that!" And then to have divested himself of his possessions and followed Jesus. But this particular story doesn't have such a happy ending. Instead of renouncing his wealth with enthusiasm, the man's face fell and he went away sad and dejected.

What does this story tell us about Jesus? For one thing, it says that Jesus can ask big things of us. He can ask us to surrender "possessions" that keep us from following him and his teachings with freedom and joy: a selfish attitude, a pet theory, a specific way of doing things.

The story also says something about discontent: It's not such a bad thing after all. In fact, a little discontent in life, a little dissatisfaction with ourselves, is actually good for the soul. St. Augustine said it well when he wrote, "Our hearts are restless, Lord, until they rest in Thee."

Prayer

Jesus, anything else? That's the question I ask you—like the man in this reading. I come to you sincerely and eagerly, and I ask, "What do I still need to do to inherit eternal life?" And I hear you listing for me all the good things I'm already doing—praying, giving of myself to others, volunteering my time, sharing my goods, trying to make good moral choices.

But then I find myself asking you, "Anything else?"

Jesus, let me be open to hear your "else," no matter how big or small. Help me to see that there's always room for growth in my life, for more compassion and love. May the restlessness I sometimes feel lead me directly to you. Amen.

42. The Meaning of Achievement

Jesus looked around and said to his disciples, "How hard it is for those who have wealth to enter the kingdom of God."
                                                    Mark 10:23-27

Reflection

Mark tells us that Jesus' disciples "were amazed at these words." Why the amazement? Because, according to Jewish belief, wealth and prosperity were signs of God's special favor. The disciples would have been taught that the wealthier the person, the easier it would be for that person to enter the kingdom of God. But Jesus had said just the opposite.

Jesus went on to explain that it was hard for anyone to enter the kingdom—wealth or no wealth. Then, to get his point across, he used hyperbole: It is easier for a camel to go through the eye of a needle than for a rich person to enter God's kingdom. Upon hearing this, the disciples were "exceedingly astonished." Jesus' words were too much to take. In frustration they asked, "Then who can be saved?"

Their question gave Jesus the opportunity to impart his real lesson. Who can be saved? By human effort alone—no one. By the power of God—anyone. Salvation is not a result of our human efforts; it is not the result of human achievement. It is a free gift from God. We do not earn entrance into God's kingdom; we receive it as gift. It is God's love that makes "all things possible."

A passage such as this should raise questions for us as teachers. What role does achievement play in our classes? Is it the "end all," or is there room for other values— cooperation, contemplation, play? Are we somehow communicating to our students the false impression that God's love is something to be earned or merited?

On another level, what "possessions" are we preoccupied with? Do we take time in our lives to be "exceedingly astonished" by Jesus' teachings?

Prayer

Jesus, I get caught up with achievement—with my own achievement and with that of my students.

Sometimes I get too caught up with the small accomplishments in my life, too preoccupied with them—or sometimes with pride. I forget the role God and other people played in many of my successes.

Jesus, give me new insights into the value and meaning of human achievement. Let me keep it in proper perspective. Let me see more in my students than what they achieve in my class. And help me to impart to them the right attitude toward that which they earn through hard work and that which they receive as a gift.

And, Jesus, encourage me to regularly take stock of my possessions—material and otherwise—which could hold me back from following you with my whole heart. Continue to do impossible things in my life, to "exceedingly astonish" me with your love. Amen.

43. What's in It for Us?

Peter began to say to him, "We have given up every-thing and followed you."   Mark 10:28–31

Reflection

Most teachers know how important rewards are. We reward students for all kinds of things: for being on time, for paying attention, for doing homework well, for behaving in a civilized manner. And the rewards we give to our students take many forms—from an affirming word to an extra recess, from a big smile to an "A+."

Expecting to be rewarded for certain actions seems to be a natural tendency in human beings. And it's something we see at play even in the disciples of Jesus. It was Peter who brought up the subject of being rewarded. He said to Jesus, "We have given up everything and followed you." By calling Jesus' attention to this fact, Peter was really asking, "What about us? What's in it for us?"

We don't know for sure exactly what each apostle had left behind to follow Jesus. We don't know how great their sacrifices may have been. Someone once remarked that Peter didn't really give up that much to follow Jesus: a couple of leaky boats perhaps, or maybe a few torn nets. But notice that Jesus didn't downplay the sacrifices each apostle had made for him. Rather, he assured them that they would be rewarded for the renunciations they'd made to follow him. And they would be rewarded not only in the next life, but also in their present lives.

What do we leave behind to follow Jesus? What sacrifices do we make for him? They may be big ones: generously sharing our resources with others, forsaking an unhealthy relationship, doing without something for another's sake. Or they may be small: attending Mass every week, being faithful to prayer each day, letting someone else have his or her way in a small matter.

Jesus insisted that his followers would be rewarded in this life. This should cause us to ask what rewards we are receiving right now for following Jesus: a good conscience, happiness and joy, fellowship with other believers, a sense of purpose and meaning in life, the nourishment of prayer and the sacraments. In short, if we really try to follow Jesus, we'll discover that there's a lot in it for us!

Prayer

Jesus, what's in it for us? That's a question my students ask me all the time: "If I do my homework, what will my reward be? If I behave, how will you pay me back? If I work hard in school, what will I get out of it?"

And if I'm really honest with myself, I must admit that I sometimes ask you the same question: "If I keep the commandments, what will my reward be? If I behave in a Christian way, how will you pay me back? If I work hard all my life, what will I get out of it?"

Jesus, help me to continue to make the sacrifices necessary to follow you—the big ones, the little ones, and all the ones in between. And help me to make these sacrifices willingly and cheerfully. Give me a greater appreciation of the rewards I'm already receiving for being not only a Christian, but a Christian educator. How lucky I am to be a follower of yours! Amen.

44. I Want to See

On hearing that it was Jesus of Nazareth, he began to cry out and say, "Jesus, son of David, have pity on me."
Mark 10:46–52

Reflection

The blind man in this story had a name, Bartimaeus. In Mark's gospel he was one of the few people Jesus cured who had a name. And although he was blind, he sensed something unusual about the particular crowd that day. When he asked, "What's going on?" the people told him, "It's Jesus of Nazareth passing through."

Immediately Bartimaeus cried out, "Jesus, son of David, have pity on me!" He must have created quite a scene with his cries, for some of the people around him told him in no uncertain terms to shut up. But Bartimaeus would not be silenced. His need for Jesus far outweighed his sense of propriety. The more the people told him to be silent, the louder he cried out, "Son of David, have pity on me!" His carryings on worked; Jesus stopped and instructed someone to tell Bartimaeus to come to him.

When Bartimaeus got word that Jesus wanted to see him, he threw his cloak aside, jumped up off the ground, and ran to Jesus. Talk about eagerness! He wanted nothing to interfere with his rush toward Jesus—so he got rid of potentially inhibiting clothing. And he didn't get up slowly, he sprang up instantly.

Then Jesus asked a rather strange question: "What do you want me to do for you?" And if we were Bartimaeus, we might have been tempted to yell back, "You mean you can't SEE what I want?" But Bartimaeus, far too much in touch with his need, answered Jesus' question unhesitatingly, "Master, I want to see." And immediately he was cured. Then Jesus reminded him (and us): "Your faith has saved you." Bartimaeus wasn't cured because he made a fuss. He was cured because his fuss was the outpouring of his faith.

Jesus comes to me every day with the question, "What do you want me to do for you?" Sometimes I am tempted to ask for foolish things: "Jesus, I want every lesson to be perfect!" Or, "I want to see visible results of my teaching." Or, "Jesus, can you make so-and-so in my class behave? "

But there's really only one thing we need to ask Jesus for—the same thing Bartimaeus asked for. We should ask that we may see potential in every single one of the students we teach. That we may see faith and goodwill in our friends and co-workers. And, most of all, that we may see Jesus walking among the crowds in our city, our town, our parish, our room.

Prayer

Jesus, I want to see. Cure me of my blindness, my nearsightedness, my lack of vision. Help me to see what really matters, what is really there. Where there is selfishness, let me see the doubt. Where there is cockiness, let me see the hurt. Where there is animosity, let me see the fear.

Jesus, help me to be so in touch with my needs that I bring them to your attention effortlessly and without shame. Help me to cast aside whatever inhibits me from running to you. May my faith in you be so alive that I see you in every crowded day. Amen.

45. Hosanna! Help Us!

"Go into the village opposite you, and immediately on entering it, you will find a colt tethered on which no one has ever sat."   Mark 11:1–10

Reflection

Mark's version of Jesus' entrance into Jerusalem is a little more subdued than that of the other gospel writers. The other evangelists described huge crowds triumphantly waving palm branches and calling Jesus "King"—almost something of a military victory parade. Mark, on the other hand, described a rather small gathering of people spreading "leafy branches they had cut from the fields."

We Christians view this event from a different perspective than Jesus' contemporaries did. We see this entry into Jerusalem as the solemn entry of the Messiah into the Holy City, where he will suffer, die, and rise again. But to the people of Jesus' day, a man riding into the city on a donkey would not have been that unusual.

Mark depicted Jesus taking care of the details for his entry into the city. This fact reinforces one of Mark's major themes: The events in the last days of Jesus' life did not happen by mere chance. They did not come unexpectedly. Jesus was somehow actively involved in their execution. To a certain extent, he was in charge of his fate.

A military leader would have ridden into the city on a horse. Jesus opted for a colt or a donkey—the mode of travel for a religious leader. The people cried out, "Hosanna!" which means, "Help us!" Jesus would indeed help the people—but in a way they (and we) could never have imagined: by suffering, dying, and rising again.

This passage highlights the difference between what seemed to be and what was. It seemed that Jesus was on the road to success; in reality he was on the road to failure. But what seemed to be failure was actually success in its fullest sense. As someone once wrote, "How little do they see what is, who frame their hasty judgments upon that which seems."

Prayer

Jesus, Hosanna! Help us! Help me! Help me to look beyond what seems to be to what actually is. Give me the patience to withhold judgment, to give people the benefit of the doubt, to allow things time to develop, to wait things out.

And, Jesus, give me the courage to go to places I would rather not go—to the Jerusalems of my life: a difficult class, a tense parent conference, an exhausting faculty meeting.

And finally, Jesus, open my ears to the cries of "Hosanna! Help us!" that I may hear today—at home, in school, on the street, in the newspaper, wherever. Amen.

46. Is It Okay to Get Angry?

He overturned the tables of the money changers and the seats of those who were selling doves.

Mark 11:15–18

Reflection

For far too long we teachers have been made to feel that it is wrong to get angry in class. "Above all things be patient—like Jesus was!" we were sometimes instructed. So this particular story of the cleansing of the temple comes as something of a surprise, for it shows us the gentle, patient, and compassionate Jesus "losing his cool."

The cleansing of the temple probably took place in the outer area of the temple—the court of the gentiles. This is where animals were sold for sacrifice and the money-changers changed the Greek and Roman coins of the pilgrims into Jewish and Tyrian coins, which alone could be used to pay the temple tax. It had to have been a wild, congested, and smelly place. And into it walked Jesus, who overturned the tables and shooed the people and animals out.

Why did Jesus do this? The answer may lie in verse 17: "My house shall be called a house of prayer for all people." Jesus seemed to have objected to the kind of prayer or worship that was going on in the temple. Perhaps he was taking exception to the fact that prayer had been reduced to ritualistic practices, and that the temple had become "a den of thieves." This phrase is straight out of the book of Jeremiah, and it refers to the place where thieves retreated for safety after robbing people. Jesus' words were not so much directed against dishonest business practices that may have been going on inside the temple; more likely, he was rejecting the notion that people could do all kinds of evil deeds outside the temple and then retreat to the confines of the temple for safety. In other words, temple prayer (or worship) is not some sort of magic trick that has no relationship to our deeds outside the temple. On the contrary, prayer and worship are intimately linked with our deeds.

Jesus drew a comparison between the temple and himself. The new "place" of salvation was no longer a mere building. It was a person—Jesus himself. The chief priests and scribes, upon hearing of Jesus' prophetic gesture in the temple, were determined more than ever to get rid of him.

Jesus had upset more than just tables.

Prayer

Jesus, please give me some of your daring, some of your energy, to fight against the injustices of my own time and place. Give me, too, a right sense of prayer and worship— one that goes far beyond magic formulas and external rituals. One that is intimately wedded to the choices I make and the deeds I do.

And finally, Jesus, cleanse my life. Come into my classes and drive out the fear and suspicion you may find there. Come into my home and drive out the hurts and anxieties dwelling there. And come into my heart and drive out the selfishness and despair lurking there. Amen.

47. About Paying Tribute

*They sent some Pharisees and Herodians to him to en-
snare him in his speech.*   Mark 12:13-17

Reflection

Once again we see Jesus "at odds" with the religious
leaders of his day. This time representatives from two different groups, the Pharisees and Herodians, went to Jesus
with the specific intention "to snare him in his speech." We
can safely assume that they had carefully planned their at-
tack.

They began by flattering Jesus, praising him for his honesty and integrity. Although they were out to destroy Jesus,
what they said about him ironically was complimentary
and perfectly true. As the old saying puts it, even the devil
speaks the truth when the truth is to his advantage!

Jesus, not fooled by their flattery, listened to their question: "Is it lawful to pay the census tax to Caesar or not?"
This tax was probably the head-tax that the Romans made
everyone pay. It was a tax bitterly resented by the Jews. In
fact, some Jews felt it was morally wrong for them to pay such
tribute to an earthly king when their only "king" was God.

The question was a clever one. For if Jesus told them not
to pay the tax, he would have been in trouble with the
Romans. And if he told them they should pay the tax, he'd
have been in trouble with the Jews. It seemed like a no-win
situation for Jesus.

But Jesus proved himself to be even more clever than his
enemies. First, he made it clear to them that he knew their
question was a setup. He said to them, "Why are you testing

me?" Then he asked them for a Roman coin. This is interesting because it meant that Jesus probably didn't have one. But his interrogators did, for one of them handed him a coin. What were they doing with a Roman coin, we might ask?

Jesus took the coin, a denarius—a silver coin comparable to a day's wages—and held it up. "Whose image and inscription is this?" he asked. They replied, "Caesar's." And then Jesus uttered those brilliant words: "Repay to Caesar what belongs to Caesar and to God what belongs to God." Hearing such an answer, even these enemies of Jesus "were utterly amazed at him."

In one short sentence Jesus gave us a remarkable principle for living—an amazingly balanced one. He refused to side with those individuals who saw this world (represented by Caesar) as unimportant or even evil. This world does have valid claims on us. But God has claims, too. And the challenge in life lies in discerning where our obligations lie.

Prayer

Jesus, help me in my rendering. Help me to render to Caesar what belongs to Caesar. Help me to assume my responsibilities to my local community, my state, my country, my world. Give me a positive attitude toward the things of earth, and help me to instill into my students a similar involvement in and a love for this life.

And help me in my rendering to God. Help me to assume the responsibility for my spiritual growth and moral development. And if there's ever a conflict between my obligations to God and my obligations to Caesar, give me the courage to stand with my God.

And, Jesus, let me never forget in whose image I am made. Amen.

48. Love God, Love Others

"Which is the first of all the commandments?"

Mark 12:28-34

Reflection

Throughout Mark's gospel, the scribes and Pharisees get a "bum rap." They come off as the bad guys. But this passage reveals that even among the scribes and Pharisees there were some admirers of Jesus. And Jesus admired a few of them, too.

The scribe in this story was impressed with the way Jesus answered his interrogators. This prompted the man to ask Jesus his own question which—unlike the questions of some of the scribes—was not meant to put Jesus on the spot. The question was the result of the man's sincere desire to learn what Jesus had to say.

"Which is the first of all the commandments?" the scribe asked. The question was one that was frequently debated among rabbis. Jesus began his answer by citing the opening formula of the Shema, the creed found in Deuteronomy that every Jewish man recited twice a day: "You shall love the Lord your God with all your heart, with all your soul, with all your mind, and with all your strength."

But Jesus didn't stop there. He connected this commandment with another one found in Leviticus: "You shall love your neighbor as yourself." The scribe asked for one commandment; Jesus responded by giving him two. Or, more to the point, Jesus combined the two separate commandments into one: Love God, love others. It's as simple (and as profound) as that!

The scribe seemed delighted with Jesus' response. He

couldn't have agreed more. In fact, he added that true love "is worth more than all burnt offerings and sacrifices." Now it was Jesus' turn to be impressed. He said to the man, "You are not far from the kingdom of God."

This passage should raise some vital questions for us about how we live our lives. Do we stereotype individuals? Does the statement "All scribes are bad" translate into our lives in any way? ("All second graders are babies, all teenagers are selfish, all administrators are unfeeling . . .") How successful are we in joining the two most important commandments into one in our daily lives? In what ways are we encouraging our students to do the same?

Prayer

Jesus, you said, "Love God, love others." It's really very simple after all, isn't it? Then why do I find it so hard to do at times? Why is it often so easy for me to love God and so difficult for me to love specific people God puts into my life?

Jesus, you knew how hard it was to love certain individuals. You knew what a challenge it was not to stereotype people, not to label them as "enemy." Help me to see people for who they really are—as you did. Help me to relate to them one-on-one, one day at a time.

Let my deep love for you overflow into my sincere affection for others. And let my love for others be an irrefutable sign of my love for you. Amen.

49. I Love This Poor Widow

He sat down opposite the treasury and observed how the crowd put money into the treasury.   Mark 12:41-44

Reflection

"We learn by doing," the old adage says. That's true. But we also learn by observing. And that's just what Jesus did in this passage. He stopped his teaching, sat down in the temple courtyard, and just observed what was going on. Do we as teachers take enough time to observe what's going on around us? We probably could learn a few things by doing so!

Jesus sat down "opposite the treasury." The treasury probably refers to the thirteen trumpet-shaped collection boxes that were located around the outer court of the temple. Jesus noticed that the wealthy "put in large sums" of money. "How generous!" we're tempted to say. But then a poor widow came and dropped in "two small coins worth a few cents." In all likelihood, the coins were copper, the smallest coins in circulation at that time. They were, at face value, an insignificant amount of money—practically worthless.

Yet Jesus called attention to the woman's contribution. He told his disciples, "This poor widow put in more than all the other contributions." How could this be? Jesus explained that the wealthy had given "from their surplus wealth," but she "from her poverty, has contributed all she had." And to really emphasize the magnitude of her generosity, Jesus added that she had given her "whole livelihood."

Few of us can read this story without being deeply touched by it. How sensitive Jesus was to have noticed this poor widow's contribution. How perceptive he was to have grasped the immensity of her gift. Jesus once again looked beyond appearances and saw what really was. He delved beneath the obvious and discovered the truth.

How good are we at doing the same thing? Do we take sufficient time before coming to conclusions? Do we look beyond mere appearances? Do we delve beneath the surface of the happenings of our day? Do we lead our students to see that there's always more to life than meets the eye?

The widow in this story should be an inspiration and a consolation for us, for we all have times when we feel very poor, inadequate, even impoverished. But she reminds us: It's not how much you give that matters—as long as you give your all.

Prayer

Jesus, I love this poor widow. She came almost unnoticed to the collection box and humbly dropped in her two tiny coins. But the clamor those coins made continues to reverberate throughout the world some 2,000 years later.

Jesus, teach me to be more generous—like her. Teach me to give not only my money, but (more importantly and often harder) my time, my talents, my ideas. And help me to find creative ways to encourage a similar generosity in my students.

And help me to observe more. To take the time to look beyond appearances, to look beneath the surface. Let me never be content with the obvious. Rather, encourage me to seek the truth. Amen.

50. Help Me Break My Alabaster Jar

A woman came in with an alabaster jar of perfumed oil, costly genuine spikenard.   Mark 14:3–9

Reflection

Jesus was reclining at the home of Simon the leper. Suddenly an unnamed woman came in—uninvited. She went directly to Jesus and, in full view of all, dramatically displayed her love and affection for him by breaking a jar of costly perfume and anointing his head with it. The woman must have shocked Simon and his guests greatly, for no one moved to stop her or to escort her forcibly from the room. Instead, they sat as if stunned by what she was doing.

Clearly the woman's display of affection was extreme. Mark tells us that she broke the alabaster jar. She held none of the perfume back. And the perfume was very expensive—worth a year's wages!

Simon and his guests were appalled by what she had done. "What a waste!" they mumbled to each other. Then, as if to justify their criticism of her, they expressed their concern that the perfume had not been sold and the money given to the poor. Their negative feelings toward the woman must have permeated the room as much as the fragrance of the perfume did.

Jesus sensed their animosity. He came to the woman's defense with the words, "Let her alone!" We sense the anger that was in his voice when he asked, "Why do you make trouble for her?" Then, to show that his view of the woman's actions was diametrically opposed to their view, he said, "She has done a good thing for me!"

Then he said, "The poor you will always have with you." Certainly Jesus was not saying that poverty is something we should accept as inevitable. His next words clarify what he meant: "But you will not always have me." Jesus was speaking of his impending death. No one is more poor than the person who is about to die. The guests were concerned about the nebulous poor that were "somewhere out there." But this uninvited guest had showed her concern for Jesus, the poor one in their very midst.

How daring this woman was! She broke into something of an "exclusive men's club" to find Jesus. She withstood hatred and derision to show affection for a man she loved and admired. And how daring Jesus was to allow a woman to touch him in public in such an intimate way.

How daring am I in letting my convictions show—in my family, my classes, my local community? How extravagant is my love for God and others?

Prayer

Jesus, help me break my alabaster jar! Help me, like that anonymous woman, to live my convictions and to let those convictions find concrete expression in outward gesture.

Let me share this woman's love for you—a love so strong that she boldly crashed a party; a love so trusting that she approached you unhesitatingly; a love so sensitive that she alone detected your dire need; a love so extravagant that she "wasted" all she had on you.

Jesus, help me to pour out my love on others—especially the "poor" I will meet today. Amen.

51. An Imperfect World

"I say to you, one of you will betray me, one who is eating with me. "   Mark 14:17-21

Reflection

I have a friend who, whenever anything goes wrong for him, recites to himself, "I live in an imperfect world, I live in an imperfect world." He claims such a reminder actually lessens his stress and anguish.

"We live in an imperfect world." Such a statement could well be the theme for this particular gospel passage. For while Jesus reclined at his table with his twelve apostles—celebrating the beautiful feast of Passover—in their midst sat one who was about to hand Jesus over to his enemies.

But let's look at some of the dynamics of this passage. Jesus knew Judas was about to betray him. Some scripture scholars see Jesus' words to the apostles as his final appeal to Judas to reconsider what he was about to do. Yet, even though Jesus knew what Judas was up to, he did nothing to stop him. And he could have!

The other apostles, meanwhile, were stunned by Jesus' announcement. Evidently they had not detected Judas' treachery at all. Their only response was, "Surely it's not me, is it?" Their question was tinged with irony. For although the other eleven were not going to directly hand Jesus over to his enemies as Judas did, they would nonetheless betray him in their own way—by running away and deserting him.

This passage is a sobering one. We might even feel uncomfortable reading it, let alone reflecting on it. It's a part of the gospel we'd prefer to skip. In fact, we might prefer to skip the entire passion narrative. For what's written here strikes very close to home. Judas and the other eleven apostles remind us that we are all capable of betraying Jesus—even those of us who consider ourselves his close friends.

We live in an imperfect world. And we teachers teach in an imperfect world, too. Have I accepted this fact? Do I allow my students to make mistakes—even serious ones? Do I allow myself to make mistakes—even in front of my students? Am I faithful to the teachings of Jesus or do I "betray him" in small ways—by questionable compromises, by a lack of focus, or even by silence?

Prayer

Jesus, we live in an imperfect world. I know this, but sometimes I live as if I didn't. These are the times I put myself down for not being better, wiser, kinder. Give me the grace to accept myself with all my imperfections, as well as all my gifts.

And help me to accept the imperfections in others—especially my students. In my efforts to teach them, let me never forget to be understanding. In my efforts to set high standards, let me never forget to allow room for mistakes. In my efforts to challenge them, let me never forget to be compassionate.

Jesus, may I never betray you by what I teach, say, or do. Give me the courage at every Eucharist to ask you, "Am I betraying you in any way, Lord?" Amen.

52. Hello Has the Last Word

While they were eating, he took bread, said the blessing, broke it, and gave it to them, and said, "Take it, this is my body."   Mark 14:22-26

Reflection

In his book, *Flowers in the Desert*, Demetrius Dumm, OSB, wrote a beautiful section entitled "Hello and Goodbye." In essence it says that "hello" is ordinarily a joyful word, but "goodbye" is often tinged with pain and sorrow. No matter how many times we say hello, we know that goodbye conquers in the end—especially the goodbye we all must say at death. "It appears that death has the last word," Dumm wrote. "But that is only an appearance." Jesus shows us "that death is . . . conquered by life in the victory of Resurrection. That means that Hello has the last word."

In the above passage Jesus said goodbye to his apostles. But before he left them, he gave them a gift of incomparable worth: the Eucharist. No doubt they comprehended very little of what he was doing at the time. (Even 2,000 years later we have not yet fully grasped its paramount significance, have we?)

Mark tells us that Jesus "took bread," "blessed," "broke," and "gave" it to his disciples. These words are the same words Mark uses in both accounts of the multiplication of the loaves. The disciples had not understood the significance of those miracles, but Jesus would finally reveal the mystery to them.

Mark's description of the last supper reflects the way the Eucharist was already celebrated in the early Christian community. We see variations of the meal in other sections of the New Testament, which tells us that there were variations and changes in the way the Eucharist was celebrated throughout those early years. That fact should remind us that periodic changes in the way we celebrate the eucharistic liturgy have always been a tradition in the church.

The description of the first Eucharist is a beautiful one. On the eve of his death, Jesus was focused on others. As he was about to end his earthly journey, he gave us a magnificent gift to nourish us in our journey through life. As we read this passage, we can only humbly whisper our thanksgiving.

Prayer

Jesus, "Hello has the last word," doesn't it? For as you were about to die, to utter your final goodbye, all you talked about was meeting again—saying hello at the heavenly banquet.

Give me the wisdom to look beyond the many goodbyes of my life—to people I've loved, to places I've enjoyed, to students I've taught—and to believe in the ultimate hello. And, on another level, help me to say goodbye to behaviors that are unhealthy, to desires that are selfish, to activities that are no longer necessary or possible.

And, Jesus, how can I ever thank you enough for the gift of the Eucharist? I can't! But may my frequent reception of this sacrament be one small sign of my immeasurable gratitude. And may your Eucharist continue to nourish me on my journey toward the kingdom—the place of eternal hello. Amen.

53. Thank You for Gethsemane

Then they came to a place named Gethsemane, and he said to his disciples, "Sit here while I pray."

Mark 14:32–42

Reflection

What happened in Gethsemane was incredible in every way. Jesus acted as we have not seen him act before. Prior to this incident Jesus had spoken calmly about his impending death. He had largely "kept his cool," except for periodic expressions of deep emotion and an occasional flare of anger. But in Gethsemane Jesus acted in a way that was uncharacteristically anxious. At first glance, he seems to have been totally out of control. And, as we know, he had every right to be.

The word "gethsemane" means "oil press." And Jesus gave the impression that he was indeed being pressed to do something he completely recoiled from doing. He took three of his disciples with him—the same three who were witness to the raising of Jairus' daughter and to the transfiguration—but he went by himself further into the garden to pray alone. Friends, no matter how close and trusted, can journey only so far with us. John Donne said, "No man is an island." But perhaps Anne Morrow Lindbergh came closer to the truth when she wrote, "We are all islands—in a common sea." Jesus knew, as we know, that there comes a time when we experience our aloneness in terrifying and agonizing ways.

Jesus fell to the ground and prayed to God, whom he addressed as "Abba," which means, "Daddy." Even in his terror, Jesus trusted God so much that he addressed God with this endearing term. Jesus then begged Abba to "take this cup away from me." The word "cup" in the Hebrew Scriptures means punishment or retribution. There's no mistaking the fact that Jesus fully knew what kind of death was in store for him. And, in a very human way, he pleaded with God to take his suffering away.

But the most important part of Jesus' prayer was what he added next: "Not what I will, but what you will." Jesus wanted to get his own way, but only if it was also God's way. Once he was convinced that this suffering was somehow a part of God's will for him, Jesus embraced it—wholeheartedly.

Jesus was fully "awake" to what was going on. His apostles, on the other hand, were almost heartlessly unaware of his anguish and impending doom. They were "asleep" in more ways than one and Jesus warned them, "Watch and pray."

Following Jesus means more than being sincere or being nice. It means being fully "awake" to the reality of evil around us. It means praying to Abba for wisdom and strength in our struggles to overcome that evil—both within and outside of ourselves.

How do I make my students more aware of the very real world in which they live? In what ways do I exemplify the Christian attitude toward suffering and prayer?

Prayer

Jesus, thank you for Gethsemane. Thank you for what you did there. Thank you for showing me clearly and dramatically that you too experienced grave fear, that you too preferred a life without pain, a world without suffering.

But most of all, thank you for addressing God as "Abba." For reminding me that I must approach God as "Daddy," or as "Mommy," no matter what seemingly terrible things may be happening in my life.

And, Jesus, give me the courage and the trust to ask God for all my needs, to lay before God all my hopes, and to express to God how I think the world should be. But give me the courage to quickly and always add your words: "Not what I will, but what you will."

And finally, Jesus, may all my teaching reflect what you taught me in the garden of Gethsemane. Amen.

54. Your Arrest Arrests Me

Then, while he was still speaking, Judas, one of the Twelve, arrived, accompanied by a crowd with swords and clubs. . . .   Mark 14:43–52

Reflection

Mark's account of the arrest of Jesus contains several significant facts. There is no doubt that the one who handed Jesus over to his enemies was Judas. And there's a certain poignancy in Mark's use of the phrase "one of the Twelve" to describe Judas. The "crowd" that came to arrest Jesus had been sent by "the chief priests, the scribes, and the elders " —in short, the religious leaders. This crowd had clout.

Judas had arranged "a signal" with these men to indicate which man was Jesus: "The man I shall kiss is the one." A kiss was a common greeting in those days—especially from a disciple to his rabbi. As soon as Judas kissed Jesus, the crowd laid hands on Jesus and arrested him.

There is something almost comic in the arrest. The crowd had come with "swords and clubs" to get Jesus. Obviously, they had no idea what kind of a person Jesus was, or they certainly would have realized their arms were totally unnecessary. Even Jesus protested the manner of his arrest. "Have you come out as against a robber, with swords and clubs, to seize me?" he asked them. They treated Jesus as if he were a man of violence who had been hiding from them. When, in reality, he had been teaching peacefully and openly the whole while.

As soon as it became obvious that "this was it" for Jesus, his disciples deserted him. Mark calls attention to their desertion by saying not merely that they "fled," but also that "they all left him." The identity of the young man who wore the linen cloth is unclear. Someone has suggested it is Mark himself—that he wrote himself into the gospel story, much like the painters of the Middle Ages painted themselves into their religious paintings. Others maintain that the mentioning of this young man was simply Mark's way of emphasizing that Jesus' abandonment was total—so desperate were his disciples to get away that one even left his clothes behind!

We might be tempted to think that this story has little to do with our own lives. Yet maybe we should ask ourselves: Am I a person of peace even when others—including my "disciples"—use violent tactics against me? How committed am I to the person of Jesus? Like him, have I ever experienced abandonment?

Prayer

Jesus, your arrest arrests me. It stops me in my tracks. How terrifying it must have been to see that mob coming toward you—the glow of torches burning in the night and the glint of drawn swords. And how devastating it must have been to receive Judas' treacherous kiss. You were a man of peace being treated like a hoodlum, a man of love being taken for a terrorist.

Jesus, help me to be a person of peace. Let me never resort to violent tactics in my dealings with others—especially my students. Keep me faithful to your teachings. And help me to endure the feelings of abandonment I sometimes experience in my life.

Jesus, let me never leave you. For you are all to me. Amen.

55. Peter Denied You

While Peter was below in the courtyard, one of the high priest's maids came along.   Mark 14:66-72

Reflection

If we're honest with ourselves, we probably like this account of Peter's denial of Jesus. We might reason that if even Peter let Jesus down, and yet went on to be a faithful disciple, then surely there's hope for us!

We're pretty safe in concluding that this particular incident really happened. Peter was a respected leader of the early Christian community. Who would have invented a story about Peter doing such an awful thing? And if this story is true, who first told it? Wouldn't it have to have been Peter? After all, he was the only disciple present when it happened. And if he did tell the story himself, we have to marvel at his humility. As one commentator says, Peter used his own shame "as a magnet" to draw others to Christ.

The story takes place in the courtyard of the high priest's residence. Jesus was inside being interrogated. Peter was outside warming himself by the fire. We have to give Peter this much credit: He didn't totally desert Jesus like the other apostles. He had every right to "lie low" like the others, but he took his chances and followed Jesus to see what was going to happen to him.

As he warmed himself, one of the high priest's maids came along and accused Peter: "You too were with the Nazarene, Jesus." Peter's response to her was evasive. He didn't actually deny Jesus at first; he pretended he didn't understand what she was talking about and walked away into the outer court. But the maid was persistent. She followed him and announced to all the bystanders, "This guy's one of them!" This time Peter denied that he was an associate of Jesus. When he was accused a third time of being one of Jesus' followers, he completely disassociated himself from Jesus—even calling down God's wrath upon himself if he was not telling the truth.

The crowing of the rooster is an intriguing detail. Roosters were outlawed in Jerusalem, so chances are it wasn't a real rooster. But at the changing of the temple guard, trumpets were blown. The trumpets were called "gallicinium," which means "cockcrow." Perhaps this was what Peter heard at that moment. It recalled Jesus' words to him: "Before the cock crows twice you will deny me three times."

The last sentence is very moving: "He broke down and wept." Peter, fully realizing what he had done, was totally devastated.

One lesson this story teaches us is this: Peter did not earn his role as leader in the early church because he was strong and perfect. On the contrary, he was keenly aware of his weakness and imperfection. He was a sinner, but he was a forgiven sinner. It was his experience of Jesus' love and forgiveness after the resurrection that made Peter great.

It's the same with us, isn't it?

Prayer

Jesus, Peter denied you. There's no denying it. And not just once either—three times. His story moves me to indignation. But it also moves me to compassion.

The terrible thing Peter did was something of a "happy fault," for, through his denial of you, he came to experience first hand your unfathomable love and forgiveness.

And I've experienced it, too. I've experienced your forgiveness when I denied you by my words, deserted you by my deeds, betrayed you by my choices.

Jesus, help me to be more compassionate toward those who let me down, who desert me, who even betray me. And let me be more understanding when others—like my students—make mistakes or even do some pretty terrible things. Help me to forgive them. Through me, may they experience your unfathomable love and forgiveness. Amen.

56. Your Trial Was a Farce

They bound Jesus, led him away, and handed him over to Pilate.

Mark 15:1-5

Reflection

Once Jesus was arrested, events moved quickly. Prior to the event described here, Jesus was tried during the night by the Sanhedrin, the supreme court of the Jews. The Sanhedrin was composed of 71 members and presided over by the High Priest. Their verdict was reached quickly: Jesus was guilty of blasphemy. And blasphemy was punishable by death. But the powers of the Sanhedrin, though extensive, did not include the power to inflict death. The Romans, who ruled the country, reserved that power for themselves.

So, as soon as dawn came, the whole Sanhedrin marched to Pilate, the Roman procurator, with Jesus in tow. In front of Pilate they charged Jesus not with blasphemy (Pilate couldn't care less about such a religious charge), but with treason (an extremely serious political charge, and one that would grab Pilate's attention).

Pilate asked Jesus, "Are you the king of the Jews?" And Jesus replied, "You say so."

Jesus' answer was ambiguous. It neither confirmed nor denied the charge. What Jesus may have been implying was this: "Yes, I am king of the Jews—but not in the way you understand the word."

The chief priests continued to accuse Jesus of many things, but Pilate seemed unconvinced. Once again he asked Jesus (in contemporary idiom), "Don't you have anything to say for yourself?" But Jesus remained silent. From then on, silence would be the hallmark of his suffering.

Mark concluded this section with the sentence "Pilate was amazed." That's the same way the first crowds reacted to Jesus at the beginning of Mark's gospel—with amazement and astonishment. It's ironic, yet also almost fitting, that even the worldly Pilate reacted to him in the same way.

In all four gospels Pilate comes across as someone who was personally convinced of Jesus' innocence. He knew trumped up charges when he saw them. Yet he succumbed to pressure and handed Jesus over to be crucified.

What is striking is how Jesus was being used. He was a mere pawn in the game of two opposing factions, both of whom were probably equally corrupt. He was executed, not for some noble and glorious cause, but because a depraved political leader was too cowardly to stand up to the pressure of a mob.

But what is even more incredible is this: God used even these overtly evil acts of individuals to bring about salvation.

How do I demonstrate that I believe this great truth? In what ways do I teach this truth to others?

Prayer

Jesus, your trial was a farce. Your trial before the Sanhedrin was completely illegal; they tried you at night, using all kinds of false witnesses to testify against you. Their verdict of "guilty" was completely unjust. And Pilate's verdict was no better. He felt you were innocent, yet he didn't have the gumption to go against the powerful Jewish leaders or the restless mob.

Jesus, you were a victim of the legal system of your day.

That causes me to ponder the justice of our own legal system today—in my country, my state, my local community. And it causes me to reflect on the level of justice in the smaller communities of my life: my parish, my school, my classroom, my family.

Jesus, invite me to work for justice in all areas of my life. And help me to encourage my students to work for justice, too. Amen.

57. Your Passion Is All About Love

They gave him wine drugged with myrrh, but he did not take it.   Mark 15:22–32

Reflection

When reading the passion of Jesus, it is easy to get caught up in the gory details: the scourging, the crown of thorns, the nails, the blood. As important as these details are, they should not be our central focus. For the story of Jesus' passion is not so much the story of Jesus' cruel death, but the story of his enormous love. Our response to reading it shouldn't merely be "look how much he suffered," but rather, "look how much he loved."

Immediately preceding this description of the crucifixion was Mark's description of the torture Jesus endured at the hands of the Roman soldiers. The scourging was a common practice intended to weaken the victim so as to shorten the actual time the victim hung on the cross. This was not done out of a sense of pity for the victim; rather, it was done to shorten the soldiers' work day. The sooner the victim died, the sooner they got to go home.

Mark didn't describe the nailing to the cross. Perhaps he didn't need to, for his listeners would have been all too familiar with this Roman execution. The soldiers cast lots for Jesus' clothes—a symbol that Jesus had nothing left, not even the shirt on his back! The bystanders and chief priests taunted him: "Save yourself by coming down from the cross." How little they knew Jesus, whose central teaching was not save yourself, but lose yourself in loving service to others.

The crucifixion was a catastrophic event. The agonizing

pain and brutal abuse Jesus underwent leaves us speechless. But it should do more than that: It should cause us continuously to reappraise the way we are living our own lives. What place does suffering have in our lives? How much pain are we willing to endure in serving others—in our families, our teaching, our local communities? What are we willing to lose or to give up so that others may live more fully?

Prayer

Jesus, your passion is all about love. Sure, it's also about pain and suffering, but not as ends in themselves. Your suffering was a direct result of your love—that link is essential. You suffered because you loved us so much. There's no other explanation. Nothing else makes sense.

Jesus, help me to love more like you. Help me to be more willing to let go of everything, to take it to the max, to go the whole way. Remind me often that genuine love always entails some form of sacrifice, some type of suffering.

And, Jesus, let this be a lesson I teach others not solely through pictures in a book or words on a blackboard. But let me teach this lesson through the kind of person I'm trying (with your help) to become. Amen.

58. Jesus Really Died

At noon darkness came over the whole land until three in the afternoon.   Mark 15:33–41

Reflection

Mark continues to count down the hours. Jesus was nailed to the cross at nine o'clock in the morning. At noon darkness came over "the whole land." For Mark, the darkness represented the powers of evil that were battling to "snuff out" the light, that is, the powers of goodness. And they appeared to be winning.

At three o'clock, Jesus cried out in Aramaic, "My God, my God, why have you forsaken me?" The words are actually the first line of Psalm 22—a psalm that begins in desolation but ends in hope. By crying out those words, Jesus was showing that his abandonment was complete.

The bystanders misunderstood Jesus' words. (He had been misunderstood from the very beginning of Mark's gospel. It's not surprising that he was misunderstood at the end). They thought he was calling on Elijah to come and save him. One man soaked a sponge in wine and offered it to Jesus. His gesture was not necessarily a kind one. Perhaps he wanted to keep Jesus alive to see if Elijah did indeed show up. But he was too late. With a loud cry, Jesus died.

Immediately after Jesus' death, the veil in the temple sanctuary was torn in two. That was Mark's way of saying that access to God was no longer the prerogative of the Chosen people; access to God was now open to all. And, as if to underscore this truth, Mark put on the lips of a gentile centurion those beautiful words of faith, "Truly this man was the Son of God!"

And women, "second-class citizens" in both religious and political circles, now enjoyed full access to God, too, thanks to Jesus. Mark mentioned by name several of them who were present at the crucifixion. Though "looking on from a distance," they nonetheless were there when Jesus died—unlike any of Jesus' male followers. Mark says that "these women had followed [Jesus] when he was in Galilee. That phrase "follow Jesus," as we saw earlier, was synonymous with discipleship.

How closely do I follow Jesus?

Prayer

Jesus, you really suffered, you really died. You weren't playacting on Calvary. You weren't pretending to suffer. No, you truly suffered and you truly died. And your death was an agonizing one. One that was accompanied by a total sense of desolation, a complete sense of abandonment—even by God.

Jesus, I doubt that anything I've ever experienced—no matter how terrible or painful it might have been—even comes close to what you experienced on Calvary. My aches and pains, my worries and troubles, seem pretty petty next to yours. Yet I hear you say to me: "Don't minimize your pains. Don't deny your sufferings. Just hand them all over to me. For they are beautiful. They are life-giving—like my pain and suffering were."

So that's what I'm doing right now, Jesus. I'm giving you my pain. I'm giving you my suffering—especially that which is part and parcel of my ministry of teaching. Make of it something beautiful. Make of it something life-giving. Amen.

59. It's Too Good to Be True!

When the sabbath was over, Mary Magdalene, Mary, the mother of James, and Salome bought spices so that they might go and anoint him.   Mark 16:1-8

Reflection

There's a consensus among scripture scholars that Mark's gospel ends with this passage. Most agree that what follows this story was added by others considerably later. Accepting this probability, we will conclude our reflections and prayers with this passage.

The sabbath ended Saturday, at six o'clock in the evening. The women mentioned in this passage bought some spices to anoint Jesus' body for proper burial. "Very early" Sunday morning as the sun came up, they made their way to the tomb. They were concerned about rolling the stone away. According to Mark, it was "very large" and they knew they couldn't move it by themselves.

But when they arrived at the tomb, they discovered that the stone had been rolled back. Upon entering the cave-like tomb, they encountered "a young man sitting on the right side, clothed in a white robe." The man was clearly an angel, whose mission was to explain to the women what they were seeing. He began by trying to ease their amazement and (we are safe in assuming) their fear. Then he said, "You seek Jesus of Nazareth, the crucified."

The mentioning of the word "Nazareth" did two things. It positively identified Jesus (the women weren't in the wrong tomb) and it reminded us that Jesus was a real human being—one who had been born and raised in a specific small town in Galilee, which was also (not coincidentally) the home of Mark's community. The phrase "the crucified" was no longer a title of shame; it was an appellation of glory.

The angel told the women, "He has been raised; he is not here." He entrusted to the women a vital message. They were to tell Jesus' disciples and Peter that Jesus was going before them into Galilee. "There you will see him," he concluded.

Mark's gospel ends not with shouts of joy and ecstasy—as we might expect upon hearing the news of the resurrection. But it ends with three women running madly away from an empty tomb, "seized with trembling and bewilderment."

Some things are just too good to be true—or are they?

Prayer

Jesus, it's too good to be true, isn't it? The way you taught the "good news" of God's love, the way you cured the sick of their misery, the way you provided bread for the hungry, the way you suffered and died out of love. And now this: the resurrection! It's all too good to be true. Or is it?

Mark's original gospel had no accounts of "the risen you." No appearances to anyone—although your resurrection was stated unmistakably as a fact. In doing this, Mark made something clear: Your resurrection was not a mere resuscitation. You did not "come back" from the dead. You went beyond death into a new kind of life—and you were urging all of us to come to the place where you are waiting for us with the Father, Abba.

Jesus, it's all too good to be true. You're too good to be true. And yet, you are!

I stand trembling. I stand bewildered. I stand amazed. Amen.

Epilogue

Jesus, Thank You for Being My Teacher

Jesus, thank you for being my teacher. The lessons of your life and deeds give meaning to my life. They color everything I do, everything I say, everything I experience, everything I am. The story of your passion urges me to greater selfless giving, to a more patient enduring of pain and suffering for love's sake. The story of your resurrection instills in me a confident hope in good's ultimate triumph over evil, and in my own final victory over death.

Jesus, these are just some of the lessons you teach me in the gospels. And although I know I've learned these lessons many times before, I sometimes need a little review and drill. And although I often do well on your written tests, I sometimes don't do so hot in the "lab of life." Yet I know you are with me. You're on my side. And, like the good teacher that you are, you sometimes push, sometimes prod, sometimes challenge, sometimes tease, sometimes pester, sometimes coax, sometimes console. But always with love, always with compassion.

Jesus, thank you for being my teacher. And thank you for calling me to be a teacher, too. Amen.

Of Related Interest...

Teaching is Like...
Peeling Back Eggshells
Melannie Svoboda
In this book, Sister Melannie offers some 50 brief reflections that sustain enthusiasm, bolster morale, and encourage teaching as a grace-filled privilege.
ISBN: 0-89622-613-1, 120 pp, $7.95 (order M-06)

Discipline Made Easy
Positive Tips and Techniques for Religion Teachers
Sr. Kathleen Glavich
Here the author provides hundreds of tested techniques to give encouragement to volunteer catechists and wise insights to veterans.
ISBN: 0-89622-598-4, 112 pp, $7.95 (order W-46)

Tools for Teaching
Joseph Paprocki
Here is a do-it-yourself manual that offers step-by-step instructions for approaching a wide variety of catechetical challenges: planning lessons, handling discipline problems, using textbooks and teachers manuals, praying with your class, choosing appropriate student activities, and many more.
ISBN: 0-89622-726-X, 96 pp, $5.95 (order B-33)

A Teacher's Prayerbook
To Know and Love Your Students
Ginger Farry
Written by a fulltime teacher, this delightful book contains prayer poems for and about students. These prayers chronicle the joys and disappointments in the life of a teacher. Each prayer is followed by a brief reflection or questions for teachers to ponder in relation to their own students.
ISBN: 0-89622-727-8, 64 pp, $4.95 (order M-89)

Available at religious bookstores or from:

 TWENTY-THIRD PUBLICATIONS
P.O. Box 180 • Mystic, CT 06355

For a complete list of quality books and videos call:
1 - 8 0 0 - 3 2 1 - 0 4 1 1